# ASTROLOGICAL
# TEXTBOOK

## BY

# LEO DANIEL
## (DANIEL SIJAKOVIC)

**2017**

**Astrological Textbook**
**Leo Daniel**
(Daniel Sijakovic)

The information from this book was presented from the best knowledge and consciousness of the author. The author does not take responsibility for any harm, which can appear by correct or incorrect way of using the methods from this book. The book is intended for getting information and education.

ISBN 9781520546056

# CONTENT

# Planets in Astrology

When assessing a certain natal horoscope we can rightfully claim that the planets are the most important carriers of the fate and the role that the man has to play reflects through them in the strongest measure, because after all, we are only the players on the stage called Life. The better and stronger position of the planet at the moment of birth is, the easier, more pleasant and more interesting are the roles for us on the stage of life. The planets can be divided into personal (in the astronomical sense, those nearest to the planet Earth with the strongest impact on the individual) and the transcendent planets (those that are quite distant from the Earth, with the strong impact on the individual, but even stronger impact on the collective events).

## The Sun

The Sun is the central body around which all other planets move, and therefore, it is the most important figure in the sky. Although the Sun is a star, in astrology it is treated as the "main, central and very special planet." It is referred to as the God of all celestial spheres, and it symbolizes the cosmic intelligence and consciousness. All other planets may symbolically represent only one ray of sunlight or the light which it reflects. It particularly affects the character, the temperament, speaking about where the "light of life" is, at what place a man can warm up and fill up the power. Someone finds the strength in family, someone at work and in the professional career, and someone in the company and numerous contacts. If the Sun is well placed at the moment of birth, it gives vitality, shine and the life energy. It particularly affects physical appearance, health and constitution, and it talks wholly about the way a person presents himself/herself to the people and what type of energy he/she carries (strength, courage, dignity or weak energy, indulgence and weak character). The position of the Sun in some sign can testify about creative preferences, but if it is well placed it gives courage, energy, good health, pride, generosity and the need for success. A person with the well-placed Sun in the sign and the aspects, easily achieves high positions, becomes favorite and respected, maintains good relations with others (especially with the elderly and the weak), being generous and protective. However, the desire for the domination can be emphasized, which may be harmful for the personal relationships and cause a lot of suffering. The strongly placed Sun at the moment of birth is about the potentially powerful people, authorities, kings, high positions and titles. The people with the strong Sun spread joy and warmth around themselves; they were born as leaders. If the Sun is strong, father can be healthy and a man of strong character (which is not obligatory), bosses and superiors will assist the person and influence his/her development and rise, the person will be ready to forgive, protect others and give love selflessly. If the Sun is weak in the sign and aspects, pride and vanity could be awakened, and the person becomes obnoxious, overbearing and arrogant, and achieves everything with the great effort and hard work. The egoism, envy, avarice, excessive ambition, arrogance and bad character can also be developed.

The sun rules the sign of Leo, in which it shows its full strength, and it is exalted (enthusiastically and with great satisfaction) in the sign of Aries. In other signs of the Zodiac the Sun reacts differently depending on the fields and aspects that it forms towards the other planets. The Sun doesn't like to be placed in the signs of Libra and Aquarius in which it is extremely weak. The strong and the well-placed Sun is the great privilege in the life of any man. It would be good if at the moment of birth the Sun was placed in the 1st, 5th, 9th, 10th and 11th house of the horoscope (even if it was in weak houses it clarifies, strengthens and improves the weak field of life and protects from diseases and enemies). So, if your Sun is not placed in the first field of the horoscope, it doesn't mean that you will not be strong, nor does it say that you will be unsuccessful and sick. According to the belief of the Hindu astrologers, the Sun corresponds to the eastern side of the world, and the gold, rubies and red gemstones are related to it.

Looking at the Sun from the angle of astromedicine we can say that it rules the heart, complete bloodstream and spine. It also rules the right eye in men, and the left in women. If at the time of birth the Sun is badly placed, a person can lose hair early and suffer from the diseases of neck, stomach, bloodstream and appendicitis. The combination of the Sun and Mars gives strong energy, optimism, but it can also contribute to the pains and diseases of bones, muscles, heart and spine. It is a frequent combination in athletes, brave and enterprising people. Sexual needs can be large, but it also depends on the rest of the horoscope. In conjunction with Saturn (especially in conjunction and stressful aspects), the Sun suffers as well as the life areas over which it governs; it contributes to the occasional or chronic pain, or prepares a man to all sorts of obstacles, it teaches a man to tolerate all restrictions, to patience and humility. In conjunction with Venus, Mercury and Jupiter, it provides good connections, talents and different favorable options, depending on the rest of the horoscope. Any planet that finds itself near the Sun can be permanently damaged or burned. In other words, it will always show weakness and sensitivity in difficult transits and it will always react in the same gentle way. Let us imagine that a man suffers from severe burns. He will always wear scars from burns on his body, whether the burns cause pain or make it impossible for him to do a certain job, the suffering will always exist as well as the memory of the same. Such a thing is also valid for the planet - if it finds itself close to the Sun it cannot always provide the expected (depending on its governance), and in some moments it creates the chronic pain and it is always sensitive to the transits. However, the other relationships and links should be assessed, too. For example, if the Sun is in conjunction with Jupiter (this is a friendly combination), and the same Jupiter rules the very favorable houses (for example the 4th and the 9th), then the combustion will not be assessed as a difficult and unfavorable, but the listed houses will be strengthened by this contact, and the beneficial effects will be transferred to the 4th and the 9th field. If you find this conjunction in the 10th house it will also influence the job and career positively, the health of the father, mother, and good opportunities for the independent business and career, the health of the born and his children. But, if instead of Jupiter you find Saturn in conjunction with the Sun (hostile combination), then both planets will suffer badly, the Sun will severely damage Saturn and all the fields which it connects, and as it is not possible to win Saturn and debilitate it completely, it will just keep giving back the malignant influence to the Sun and it will reduce everything that the Sun rules, and in the domino effect it will weaken the health of father, honor, status, career, cause severe damage to bones, muscles and bloodstream and finally to the mother (if the conjunction occurred in the same place as in the previous case). On the other hand, the owner of the horoscope must work hard and prove himself by going to extremes and above the average; he must always be modest and humble, and tolerate his fate well. Even when he did something extraordinary, the others would wisely keep silent and swallow saliva. Everything possible will be used against the owner of the horoscope; he will always have to try over and over again. He will work hard, often without respite, without awards, commendations, and if he decides to travel somewhere to rest, he would again be called to work. However, if the same conjunction of the Sun and Saturn finds itself in the sign of Cancer or Leo, then the maleficence would grow even more; if Saturn is in its own sign, for example. In Aquarius, it will not suffer much from the proximity of the Sun and such a combination may help, especially if the said two planets take good positions and principalities in the horoscope. The realization of something would take time and hard work, but the success would follow. There are many combinations that include or exclude the above mentioned, but it will not always be easy to understand the network of relationships, because you need to know more than 1,000 planetary combinations and connections at the same time. This can sometimes create serious confusion, especially when you decide to make some money of the interpretation of the horoscope. You will soon realize that you have not been practicing enough. Anyway, these are just brief remarks on the influence of the Sun in relation to other planets.

Day of the week corresponding to the Sun: Sunday.

Astrosymbolism of the Sun: all the important and famous people, actors, celebrities, kings, managers, authorities, emperors, men, child, father, sunflower, chamomile, grapefruit, animals of the feline, sports, games, monarch, wiseman, professor, golden objects, grandeur, brilliance, courage, pride, greatness, generosity, boastfulness etc.

The Sun in mythology: in Greek mythology, the god of the Sun is Helios. He is the son of the Titan Hyperion and the Titaness Theia, the brother of Selene and Eos (the goddess of the morning blushes).

The Sun in astronomy: the Sun is mainly composed of hydrogen and helium, the temperature of the layer that we can see is about 6000 degrees Celsius, while the interior can reach several million degrees Celsius. The Sun runs one degree per day, it rules one zodiacal sign per month, and it runs the entire Zodiac per year.

## The Moon

The Moon is known to the people mostly for having the ebbs and tides, which is in the largest part caused by its gravity. It is occasionally mentioned that during the full Moon the mental hospitals are full of weirdoes who identify with Napoleon or some other historical figure; the people are sensitive, drink more and tend to crime and strange behavior. That's about all we know about the Moon. In addition to the fact that it is a natural Earth satellite, which is about 380 thousand kilometers away, it is especially important in astrology because, according to some authorities, it represents the feminine principle, the finest and the most subtle part of every human. The fact that it is so sensitive creates an eruption of emotions in a man that makes him susceptible to external developments. It represents the mind in the first place, and then the feelings that arise as a result of a healthy or a sick mind. The world that surrounds us and the one we create depends on the power of the Moon. In the West the astrologer uses its position to comprehend and decipher whether the client loves the dim lights or not and what his supposed feelings are. And then, if it happens that the Moon is strong in the natal chart - then the man is automatically very caring, gentle and attentive, and if it is weak - the astrologer estimates that he has come across a bad man who has no soul and no heart for others, the furious tyrant and a misogynist. And if the Moon is, God forbid, in the sign of Scorpio or Capricorn - then it is undoubtedly like that and much more than that. So, these people and the like have no chance in life. However, although everything is like this, we find that most murderers, criminals, thieves and ruthless people live with the Moon in the sign of Pisces. If we look at the charts of German SS officers, again we do not find the Moon in Scorpio, or we encounter it more frequently in other signs that describe the "divine love and harmony." Therefore, be careful when making judgments about people and when, on the basis of the moment of birth, you evaluate their lives. You need to be very clever and wise, which is often not the case.

The Moon principle is particularly conspicuous even when a child is still in the womb, because the mother transmits the encoded information concerning his feelings, fears, growing up, the ability to protect himself from the outside world, as well as to love, to feel, to provide support and give back all the love and attention. Therefore, it is responsible for the negative emotions, such as hatred, possessiveness and jealousy, which also belong to the feminine principle. Thus, the Moon is not made of the appearance of things and all that which can be seen, but it is made up of integuments and wrappings that every man carries hidden deep inside. These integuments are the essence of our lives, but we usually realize it only when we lose a loved one, start a family, grow old, or when our toys (money, work, fame, properties...) pass over to the hands of others (our kids, or some lucky heirs). So, the astrologer can receive the important information about the family or the genetic heritage based on the position of the Moon, the fate of the mother and what was she really like when she was pregnant (calm, gentle and loving or possessive, scared and rough, worried about the future). Further, the position of the Moon at the moment of birth can tell a lot about the childhood, growing up and collecting important data which will be used in the life of a man no matter whether he builds or demolishes, whether he defends him-self or attacks. The good position of the Moon sometimes gives a gentle, peaceful and fruitful mother, but if the op-posite is the case, it can evoke various complexes such as Oedipus's or Electra's, so we often find mothers who are in an unhealthy and strange way related to their children. The good position of the Moon gives harmonious and rich life, popularity, protection, pretty face, women's curves, good appetite, healthy sexuality, emotional stability and durability, the ability to develop closeness and empathy with people, good carers, it gives psychologists and psychi-atrists (it is often the case with the doctors, psychologists and psychiatrists that the Moon is extremely damaged in the sign and aspects, and thus represents the way to solve personal fears and problems). The position of the Moon at the moment of birth tells us about the people who come into our lives and what kind of people we attract, but the attraction is more related to how we vibrate and transmit than to how we look or how we comb our hair. So, the Moon is not solely responsible for the ability of a man to forgive others and feel compassion, as some repeat persis-tently (in practice we sometimes notice that people with the damaged Moon forgive much more), but it develops the emotional intelligence in a man which will help him go through life as light as a feather or as easy as possible, if it's possible at all. This automatically implies the forgive-ness of insults, a sense of security and closeness to all the creatures. Perhaps the true mantra for the Moon should be: "I love people and all living beings", which again implies the inability to hurt others emotionally, to hate and inflict physical pain and suffering. Although everything is like this, the pain, hatred and suffering abound. We witness that every day.

If it is well-placed in the horoscope, it can reward the man with the special charm, it can awake the maternal instinct, medium skills, artistic qualities, but otherwise it brings frequent mood swings, hysteria, anxiety and in some cases severe mental illnesses. In the male horoscope and on the basis of its position, we can see what kind of woman pleases him and what kind of woman he fantasizes about (this belongs to the domain of fun astrology).

The Moon rules the sign of Cancer, it is exalted in Taurus, and it is weak in Capricorn and Scorpio, where it creates suffering. You can say that its weak spots are Aries, Virgo and Pisces.

Moon in Business astrology: army, natural sciences, history, archeology, psychology, poetry, children's education, agriculture, trade, social nutrition, seamanship, restaurants, hotels, confectioners, bakers, milk, fish.

Moon in Astromedicine: the breasts, uterus, ovaries, left eye in men and right eye in women, abdominal pain, various psychological disorders... If a man reacts tumultuously and stressfully to everything that happens around him, the weak position of the Moon often helps tumors.

Day of the week: Monday.

Moon colors: white and silver.

Gemstones: Pearls and moonstone.

The Side of the World: Southwest.

Astrosymbolism of the Moon: plants, babies, vegetables, flowers, soul, caterer, bread, milk, waters (lake, sea, ocean), bathroom, livestock, maternal instinct, family, house, garden, memories, clairvoyance, dreams, food, nation, restlessness, anxiety, hypersensitivity, underwear, plumber, grave, bedroom, imagination, inspiration, intimate things, etc.

The Moon in mythology: Greek goddess of the Moon is Selene, and in the Roman mythology it is Luna. She fell in love with the hunter Endymion who suffered a tragic fate. Luna visited him every night to kiss him and caress him with her rays.

# The Moon in the signs of the Zodiac

*The Moon in Aries* is manifested directly, courageously, dynamically and passionately. It flares up quickly but it is capable of regaining calmness and handling its emotions in a short time. It reacts vigorously, violently and impulsively, but it is not morose or malicious. It can also speak about the problems with sinuses, ears, teeth and the dominant mother or wife. It is present in the horoscopes of the athletes, innovators, brave and determined people. In some cases it resembles the Moon in Scorpio, since it is in the sign of Mars, but it is able to pull itself together and organize quickly, and to use or discard the gained experience, if necessary, which is not the case with the Moon in Scorpio.

*The Moon in Taurus* is manifested slowly, sluggishly and materialistically. The desire for pleasure and comfort is emphasized. It can bestow a distinct fertility, a good life in the countryside and a beautiful family home. It is often a sign of abundance and good living conditions, of happiness and wealth. All this is somewhat reduced, if it is damaged by difficult aspects. It is present in the horoscopes of caterers, confectioners, chefs, hoteliers, builders, landlords, of the practical, materialistic and rich people. If, by any chance, your Moon is in Taurus and you are not a confectioner - do not worry. The same position of the Moon can also be found in any profession. Sometimes it gives certain inertia and passivity, if the ascendant is in Cancer or strongly placed elsewhere in the horoscope. It reacts strangely to everything new, queer, unusual and hasty. This is the excellent and healthy position of the Moon.

*The Moon in Gemini* reacts quickly, enthusiastically and finds its strength in a number of information, which it later simply discards. It indicates a family of teachers or the educated ancestors. A person with the Moon in Gemini doesn't feel easy in his own skin. Sometimes a love of mechanics, cars and roads is noticed. These people are fast and easy learners. They forget very quickly because of the need to adopt new information. They are often sloppy in relationships and look at life with a lot of pink. Their discussions and reflections are colored by the play games and flippancy that is not inherent in the position of the Moon in some other sign. The security is supposedly acquired through the mass of information that, ultimately, serves no purpose. All this is mitigated when the rest of the horoscope indicates the opposite. Although everything is so, one cannot say that this is a problematic position of the Moon. Once in the sign of Gemini and in good aspects - it can fulfill the wishes of each life sector it rules.

*The Moon in Cancer* is hypersensitive, which implies numerous problems and emotional injuries. It is variable and it reacts in accordance with the environment. It binds possessively to the family from which it expects much. If there are afflictions, it can develop vindictiveness and heavy reactions. Although Cancer is the place where the Moon is elevated, the people with this position are not always welcome in the society because of their volatility and hypersensitivity. A mother often lives with her child, especially if it is in the 8th house or in contact with Saturn. If it is well placed (a healthy and a strong house as well as the aspects to the benefices), it brings success, progress and good credits. As this is a sign of its main seat, it will always give more and better in the life field it rules.

*The Moon in Leo* responds enthusiastically, strongly and warmly with the need to appropriate things and privileges. It seeks constant attention and enthusiasm. It enjoys everything that the external environment brings, turbulently and clearly responding to all of this. Pride may affect the decline in popularity and conflicts with others. This position is not always the best for mother or wife. If it is present in the male horoscope it often brings a mother or a wife with no steady job or a source of income, who are not sure what their mission in life is, and what exactly they should be doing. These people are very proud and are not able to perform all jobs, nor are they able to get to grips with all of life's challenges. This can be the problem especially in the tough and poor years. This position is relieved by the emphasized Virgo in the horoscope, or the aspects of the Sun and Saturn. Although everything is so, one cannot say that the same position does not give popularity and courage. I have noticed that it is often about the successful people in high government positions. So, it is much happier in Leo than in the signs of Scorpio and Virgo. It is important to assess the rest of the horoscope.

*The Moon in Virgo* reacts arduously, uncertainly and critically, which diminishes the popularity. On the other hand it is a good indicator of the practical and analytical intellect, which can be especially useful for researchers. If afflicted, it can cause severe mental suffering, depression and the loss of self-confidence. Sometimes we encounter the strange behavior, irrational fears, avarice and criticism. During the course of my humble research I have encountered the lack of empathy for the weak and poor people. There is also the need to prolong life as much as possible, although such a position rarely creates a jovial person, a hedonist, or someone who knows what he will do with his life. In some cases there is an emphasized sense of guilt. It indicates very smart and capable ancestors, but we do not have any clear evidence for these claims. This position can sometimes cause serious suffering to the mother and women through depression, apathy and illnesses. It is rarely the sign of an optimistic, cheerful, enthusiastic and simple person. These people are often smart, but their lives are burdened with digression, unnecessary analysis, parsing things and criticism. It is found in the horoscopes of the intellectuals, doctors, psychologists, mathematicians, office workers and precocious people. However, this is not a rule, and all this should not be taken for granted. I had the opportunity to meet wonderful characters with the position of the Moon in Virgo, but there were also other factors that have aided the abovementioned. So, it is not mandatory that such a position is detrimental to the owner of the horoscope.

*The Moon in Libra* is good and it is bearable only in the first decade of Libra. It speaks of the refined spirit, the refined taste, the desire and the need for beautiful and comfortable things. Sometimes there is the accentuated need for sweets or the pursuit of artistic expression and everything that pleases the senses. The finesse is emphasized both with cold emotions hidden behind the pleasant and beautiful facade. Relationships are often marred by the dishonest presentation and lack of self-confidence. It is a good position for artists and lecturers. The Moon in Libra is capable of masking their true emotions, and therefore enjoys popularity in a society, because you can never know what they exactly feel. This allows it to come out as the winner out of many situations and spare itself further embarrassment. This position can bring social success and it is desirable in horoscopes because this world needs nice, moderate and friendly people.

*The Moon in Scorpio* is quite sensitive and intense so it attaches itself easily to the people. It creates a number of hostilities due to deep and intense relationships, which often end ingloriously. It can love deeply and possessively, and then it abandons in an effort to protect itself. The same people are easy to love, but also easy to hate. They are often responsible for those emotions themselves, and many times even their enemies are not entirely sure why they hate them. It is the erotic and passionate position of the Moon, but it is not at all the sign of love and sexual happiness and joy. So, its presence in the chart does not diminish the chances for others to be happy in bed. It has been noticed in doctors, surgeons, healers and psychiatrists, but not as a written rule. In some cases we find that it is good for the literature, writing, but not necessarily crime and erotic novels about which the fun astrology talks about. They respond well when you love them, or when you are loyal to them, because they have long memories and in this way you can buy their loyalty and faithfulness forever. This position reduces popularity and harms women or the mother, as well as the life sector which it rules. It is good for the research, esoteric sciences and astrology, while the daily life is thwarted by the numerous riots, internal and external struggles. Although it is in the sign of its decline, the Moon in Scorpio often speaks about the vital, tough, persistent and fanatical people.

*The Moon in Sagittarius* is manifested boldly, decisively, with a lot of confidence and dynamism. There is the need for immediate, strong and direct contacts devoid of hidden intentions, pathos and volatility. There is the strong belief and hope that changes depending on the spheres of influence and the new enterprise. The competitive spirit and the faith in a better tomorrow are accentuated. Although everything is so, there is the selfish need to satisfy their interests. This is the good position for lecturers, athletes and travelers. Sometimes, it speaks about the life and success abroad. This position contributes to popularity, which is often undeserved, but also to the good outlook on life and everything that it brings. The philosophy spirit can be colored by the excessive optimism and sometimes superficial knowledge which creates damage in the long run. This is the lighter and healthier position than in the previous sign, but not a guarantee for happiness, success or good health.

*The Moon in Capricorn* sometimes speaks of the humble childhood and in the later years of success and the earned riches. The rigidity, coldness and the veiled ambition are emphasized, which can be seen only by the close family members. Sometimes it speaks about the sad life of mother and the excessive attachment or constraints for the same, resulting in superficial, long and cold relations. The emotions are often blocked by the excessive introversion and planning of the future. This is a good position for the veterinarians, doctors, professors and businessmen. When other factors confirm that, we find here the refined and good taste for film, music, design and architecture. If the desires are aimed at materialistic acquiring and social success - such a position can help. In some cases the Moon in Capricorn speaks of infertility, but it depends a lot on the position of Saturn and other factors in the horoscope. Depending on the rest of the horoscope, sometimes we find the interest in astrology, tradition, roots and the old. In several cases I have encountered significant interest in the occult, especially when fixed stars are accentuated and determined, as well as the sign of Scorpio, the 12thfield or when the ruler of the Ascendant has a strong connection with the series of the 12th or the 8th. But all this should be complemented by the research and improved.

*The Moon in Aquarius* feels good in groups, collectives and other places where the community spirit is recognized. Although the Moon in Aquarius represents itself as the individual and the self-conscious, we see that it hardly functions on its own and without the great support of the others. The desire to appeal to the mass often thwarts the 'one-to-one' relationship, and in some cases it is the guarantee for the bad marriage or fragile friendships. You can also notice the progress and the acceptance of all that is the product of the collective. The refusal or rejection of the modern trends is rarely noticed. This is a good position for innovators, artists, astrologers, engineers and developers, but it can only happen if the rest of the horoscope indicates a similar connection. In the men's horoscope such a position of the Moon seeks protection of the wife or the mother. Although astrological literature mentions that they are philanthropic, the need for popularity is often noticed. The mind of those persons is restless, always facing possible new ideas, inventions and adventures. They are ready to jump out of the established patterns and repeatedly start a new life, which is good, because a person begins to age from the moment he/she becomes afraid of change.

*The Moon in Pisces* is expressed in a quiet and dreamy way, with the lack of real zeal, with the need to pull back and retrospect. It is noticed in sensitive and volatile people, and sometimes it is accentuated in artists and unusual people. It is also very common in people who suffer from depression, mental illnesses and in problematic people. One study showed that a large number of convicts, prisoners and troubled people often lived with the position of the Moon in the sign of Pisces. Due to the fact that Pisces are characterized as secret, deceptive and uncertain, it is not rare that we are deceived by people with the emphasized Pisces or that we underestimate their quality and true nature. Whoever the Moon in Pisces represents in someone's chart, you should always examine this field thoroughly. The same applies to the other dubious positions in the horoscope. If the rest of the horoscope is vital, this position contributes to the kind and polite behavior, it encourages creative and artistic potential and strengthens and develops closeness with others. Thus, it is never enough to estimate one position of the planet in order to draw conclusions.

Although the Moon can represent all of the above mentioned, the astrologers forget that it can also represent father in someone's horoscope or relatives (ruler of the 10th house), or the siblings (ruler of the 3rd house). This may help you while you surf the Internet eager to learn. Thus, the Moon is not only a mother, milk and a lamp, but also many other things.

And finally, the most important thing that concerns the Moon: **Life is a state of mind.**

You should never forget that.

## *Mercury*

With the appearance and discovery of the transcendental planets (Uranus, Neptune and Pluto) the planet Mercury was somehow suppressed and for astrologers it was the association with small things, children, youth and the technical failures of the equipment in case its gait was retrograde. Mercury has long been considered to be a planet that signifies astrology, and today it is, ostensibly, Uranus, because we live in modern times, where every day we get new versions of mobile phones, computers and other technological aids. However, people keep forgetting that the development of technology does not go hand in hand with the development of consciousness. The truth is that technology is getting better, but it is also true that a man is morally weaker, and that today, as well as thousands of years ago, we have hatred, adultery, theft and other weaknesses of the human spirit.

Healthy Mercury with the relatively strong Moon is a prerequisite for a healthy mind and head (in combination with the Moon and other factors in the horoscope). The claim that in a healthy body there is a healthy mind is suspicious, and we could rather say that in a healthy spirit there is a healthy body, because we have not seen anyone mentally weak, and at the same time bursting with health.

In the East they say that Mercury is the messenger of God, and that information is transmitted directly by the divine eminence as a man receives his messages. Thus, we can conclude that it is especially responsible for the ability to speak, intelligence, practical and abstract thinking, movement and coordination. Its good position promotes logic and thoughtful processes, allows short and long trips, good childhood, joy, play and interesting life contents, giving agility and maneuverability, thus directly affecting the practical ability and spiritual insight. People with good Mercury can easily and quickly adapt to major life changes, new situations; they easily acquire knowledge, do not suffer because of the dynamism in the family and the outside world, they are willing to learn, they are flexible and receptive. If it is weak it can donate modest intelligence, difficulty in speaking, slow or unclear linkage of things, big misconceptions, errors and omissions. This weakens the healthy humor, optimistic view of the world, education and learning. Mercury, which was damaged at the moment of birth, is one of the indicators for many mental disorders, mental weakness and poor health. It comes from the simple truth that mentally weak person cannot enjoy good health. This implies instability, kleptomania, lack of concentration, malice, slander, and often modest intelligence.

Mercury rules Gemini and Virgo, and feels particularly unwell in Sagittarius and Pisces.

Mercury rules the nervous system and lungs, and symbolically describes events from four to fourteen years of age.

Astrosymbolism of Mercury: knowledge, library, means of transport, travel, cousins, brother, child, humor, intelligence, wisdom, intellect, traffic, small things, practical objects, phone, any form of communication, books, letters, small animals, mental weakness, trade...

Mercury in business astrology: commercial, languages, small business, sales, supplies and materials, books, travels, tourism, transport, accounting, printing industry, repair, equipment, tools, medicine, therapy, job management, trade...

Mercury in mythology: Mercury in Greek mythology is represented by Hermes sent by the supreme God Zeus to be the messenger of the gods.

Here's how Mercury works depending on the sign in which it is placed.

*Mercury in Arises* is expressed imperiously, sharply, clearly and directly, without the need for beautifying things. Such an approach to life creates enemies and leads to dangerous and unfortunate situations. The need for the rhetorical speculation is emphasized, entering the discussions that necessarily require capitulation and the wisest opponent. In fact, a certain rigidity and severity of the attitudes that sometimes resemble stubbornness are noticed. Considering the fact that it decides abruptly, it often leads the Natus (born) into problems or business adventures. The power of persuasion is really tremendous with this position of Mercury (Einstein, Zola).

*Mercury in Taurus* is expressed somewhat more slowly, practically and thoroughly with a lack of abstract thinking. Sometimes we see a slow and difficult speech, as well as the strange connecting of things that gives the lack of imagination. If it is badly placed or heavily afflicted, it can reduce intelligence and make thinking processes lazy. All that changes if it is placed in the corner houses, if it builds strong aspects or if it is placed on the emphasized fixed star (Balzac).

*Mercury in Gemini* is expressed cheerfully, easily, it tends to quickly adopt and also forget things. It gives certain youthfulness in the mature years of life. Many life lessons are easily metabolized and forgotten which is quite good, if the Natus lives a turbulent, dynamic or stressful life. There is a love for books, socializing, traveling and exchanging experiences. These people are never bored and we notice a tendency towards learning, curiosity and joyful spirit. All this can be mitigated and reduced by its afflictions. The damaged Mercury in Gemini can provide a strong vanity, nervous tension and dyslexia (Richard Bach).

*Mercury in Cancer* is expressed by the need to moderate real feelings and attitudes and to create emotional intimacy with the other party. It can bring a poetic and artistic gift, as well as a serious talent for foreign languages. We see a strong and deep memory and in some cases we find ingenious and romantic people who understand some great truths of life (Tesla, Alexander Dumas).

*Mercury in Leo* is expressed warmly, cordially, theatrically, ostentatiously, with great zeal and enthusiasm. It has been noticed in the numerous popular writers (Faulkner, Hemingway, Coelho...), but also in people who are confident about their attitude, speech and reasoning. If it is placed close to the Sun it can give a pretentious nature, a braggart and the need for decoration and beautification of speech. Handwriting is often beautiful, flamboyant and skewed. There is a certain talent for art and a strong memory.

*Mercury in Virgo* is expressed cautiously, timidly, painfully, with the need that everything which is adopted has some kind of order, meaning and array. It is able to learn more and better than the others, but does not like it and does not feel good about it. It is one of the indicators of nervousness, anxiety and sometimes even depression. Definitely the strongest position of Mercury, but it is not at all easy. A gift for music and a good pitch is often noticed.

*Mercury in Libra* is expressed beautifully, steadily, warmly and insincerely. It's good for writing and working in public. It is capable of creating magic and art. These people are often good speakers and in contact with people they are very friendly and hospitable (Scott Fitzgerald).

*Mercury in Scorpio* is expressed sarcastically and ironically, the thoughts are burdened by the depth and the way of looking at the reality. This is a good position for disguises, writing and psychology. In some cases, there is the lack of tact in saying things that people cannot and do not want to hear (Flaubert, Leonardo di Caprio, John Malkovich).

*Mercury in Sagittarius* is expressed warmly, optimistically, with a wide and bright view of the world. It is often the victim of its own thoughts and decisions. If the ascendant is in Virgo, they can be of gentle health, prone to misjudgments and strange behavior. Overall, this is one jovial and optimistic nature.

*Mercury in Capricorn* is expressed cautiously without the need for decorating and shaping. The speech can be slow, difficult, infused with pessimism, clear and practical ideas. The ideas are often directed towards concrete matters and things that are useful in life. It is capable of learning, remembering and developing the life philosophy, which often relies on old and traditional values. It is particularly significant in the horoscopes of teachers, professors and educators.

*Mercury in Aquarius* is expressed freely and clearly. There is a noticeable gift for music and the need for mental compatibility and familiarity. It gives the outstanding artists, active imagination and an extraordinary talent for music (Mozart).

*Mercury in Pisces* is expressed dreamily with minor or severe speech impediments. It gives the ability for learning foreign languages and abstract thinking that is largely imbued with wrong decisions and suspicious findings. This is the weak position for strategists and researchers. It significantly affects humor, the ability for disguise, acting, imitation and spiritual discipline. Although Mercury is extremely weak in Pisces, it does not mean that the person does not possess intelligence or is unable to develop practical skills.

## Venus

Venus is the brightest and the most visible planet of the solar system. It is widely known as the Morning star because it rises and sets with the Sun. Venus is especially important because it represents more beautiful and enjoyable part of life, which includes all kinds of pleasures, joy, songs, love, lust for life and the ability to make people love each other, as well as the ability to receive love. This implies a gratuitous inner happiness that makes the world and all that is happening around us to be observed through the pink glasses and utterly harmlessly. On the other hand, it is able to attract light gains, well-being, comfort and wealth. In the East magic and demonic properties are added to Venus, because it is capable of seducing, persuading and bewitching a man. Haven't we witnessed so many times that people behave strangely in love, that a miser opens his bag, that a man leaves his family for someone's beauty, or that wars are led because of a woman, such as the Trojan war. Thus, Venus, although benign, can awaken a strong, animal eroticism, possessiveness and jealousy, and excessive desire for physical enjoyment in a man. If at the time of birth Venus was aspected stressfully and affected by other planets, it shows extremely negative properties: the marriage is bad, or entered late, the person is not capable of loving or loving back; there is an inability to stay in one relationship or in one marriage; laziness wakes up and the atypical sexual orientation, which can often be perverse, a person prefers to stay in the shade than opting for a responsible and hard work. If it is well aspected, a person easily attracts smaller or larger gains, he/she is beautiful and harmonious both outside as well as inside. The well placed Venus helps a man to be happy and satisfied even when he has little, allows him to rejoice in the sunset, in the aurora, in the ordinary and small things. A man with a good Venus can enjoy love even if his partner is neither pretty nor handsome. In the male horoscope it depicts his girlfriend or wife. It encourages the sexual attraction and is responsible for every kind of luxury, the joy of life and satisfaction. At a higher level, Venus could represent cosmic love, bliss, and the idea of "love thy neighbor as thyself." However, this is just an abstract tendency that is eventually reduced to trivial pleasures and sensual indulgence. Venus rules the reproductive organs, skin, neck, cheeks and kidneys. It rules the signs of Taurus and Libra, and it feels very weak in Virgo, Aries and Scorpio.

In business astrology Venus is responsible for the so-cio-social activities, art, architecture, designing clothes, working in hair and beauty salons, working with jewels, precious metals, jewelry, ornaments and decorative objects, fashion and public affairs.

Day of the week: Friday.

Colors: pink, white, mix of colors (colorful).

Astrosymbolism of Venus: flowers, chocolate, money, intimacy, love, warmth, friendliness, treats, toys, harmony, musical instruments, musicians, necklace, clothing, pictures, laughter, happiness, ornaments, satisfaction, courtship, passion, kinship, poetry, cakes, public places, sex, feminism, singer...

Venus rules from fourteen to twenty-two years of age.

Venus in mythology: Venus was born from the sea foam impregnated by Uranus. Today, Venus is associated with the Greek goddess of love, Aphrodite. From mythology we learn that Venus was not too loyal and that she had affairs with many lovers and gods.

*Note: If at birth your Venus was found in a weak sign or the aspects, it does not mean that you are not capable of loving or receiving love, nor is it a sign of widowhood or permanent misery. However, you'll definitely need to undergo different experiences and learn much about love, no matter whether you are a master of relationships, or a partner does not know how to respond to your giving and expectations properly. I saw a lot of wonderful people with the impaired Venus who also enjoyed good marriages. Each of them confessed that they worked hard for what they get in marriage or other relation. So be nice, love people, and be kind. You will always get the same minimum of love you gave to others, and often much more. Sometimes you will not get it from the person you gave your love to, but you will always receive it back. Venus can teach you to love everyone and everything, even if sometimes it seems that there are no good reasons for that. So, love and let somebody love you. It is not that difficult.*

## *Mars*

In Roman mythology Mars was honored as the god of war, while in Hellenistic mythology it fitted to Ares, blinded by hatred, cruelty and the desire for any kind of struggle.

Mars needs to be projected and manifested in the external, in the real and physical world, and therefore we say that it has no tact or that it functions on the completely unconscious level. It is the planet of very powerful energy. With the advent of transcendental planets (Uranus, Neptune and Pluto), modern astrologers have forgotten how unpredictable and dangerous Mars was. The planet Mars awakens courage in man, the initiative, the desire for action and active work, competitive spirit and aggressiveness. The overemphasized Mars in the horoscope makes arrogant, violent and unrelenting guys confident enough to cope with any of life's challenges, but also to cause pain and injuries to the others. Strong Mars creates a steadfast spirit, strong musculature, heavy body hair, awakens courage, aggression and the desire to win. For this reason, it is emphasized in veterans, soldiers, athletes, drivers, workers and all those who have the urge to win and progress. Mars represents the hidden earth energy of the materia that once again wants to be converted into matter. In other words, by its operations it creates a tangible work after which some kind of life criteria are created (victory in war, football or tennis match, grabbing of territory, defeating the opponents, imposing domination...). If Mars is bad, whether in the sign or in the aspects, it can create a violent nature, an aggressor or an extremely cruel man. If it is weak and in the horoscope there is no strong interest, no fuel, no passion, nothing works... That's why we say that its action is focused on a clear and specific goal. Mars rules the head and genitals, left ear, muscles, prostate... Its day of the week is Tuesday and the color is red. It occupies the south side of the world. It takes almost two years to circle the Zodiac.

Its stressful transits bring serious physical injuries and falls, violent and sudden death, life breaks and incessant struggles, conflicts and clashes, fevers, inflammation and poor health. Well placed Mars gives strong sexual appetite and great stamina, and the ability to overcome many challenges of life. Mars rules the signs of Scorpio and Aries, but their nature is completely different. It feels good in Capricorn, and it is extremely poor in Cancer or Libra in which it has a malignant influence which sooner or later must be exhibited. In business, Mars could create a good surgeon, butcher, hairdresser, chemist, technician, engineer, electrician or other practical worker. Everything related to tools, heavy machinery, hard work, industry is related to its operation. From its energy we can burn and perish or we can be extremely productive. In the horoscope it represents partners, lovers, brothers and enemies (opponents).

Mars rules the cycle of forty to fifty-six years of age.

Astrosymbolism of Mars: tools, explosives, combat, competition, courage, initiative, rage, anger, energy, inflammation, fever, athletes, construction workers, wild animals, soldiers, police, thief, all sharp objects, machines, hot foods, meat, jealousy, sarcasm, quarrelsome nature, impulsiveness, sexual appetite, libido, power...

## *Jupiter*

After the Sun, Jupiter is the largest body of our planetary system. In modern astrology Jupiter is the happiest planet, while in the Indian astrology this honor went to Venus. Jupiter, with its enormous gravity, collects asteroids that wander around the Universe, which could destroy the Earth in a split second, if only this delicate giant allowed them to pass by. It has the embodied wisdom and grace we receive in life and it is, therefore, the source of happiness, prosperity, spiritual and material progress. Astrologers believe that it is generous and that it helps a man in every sense through the growth and expansion in all directions. Jupiter represents the law and order of the Universe, and therefore, symbolizes morality, justice and goodness. Its position at the time of birth indicates the purpose - someone was born to make family, somebody learns and teaches, somebody entertains and somebody cures people. Jupiter gives us support, a good wind and sails, so the things go much better than we could have imagined. In the East Jupiter is called Guru (the one who has the knowledge and the overall wisdom), and refers to the spiritual aspirations and cosmic consciousness which lives unawake in man. However, a modern man uses Jupiter's grace for the acquisition, accumulation of wealth, the accumulation and deposition of earthly goods. In the East it is believed that its color is yellow, and in the West we say that Jupiter symbolizes the blue color. Its day is Thursday. Jupiter rules the signs of Sagittarius and Pisces, and it feels bad in Capricorn, Virgo and Gemini. It is believed that the same planet is exalted (elated and very happy) in the sign of Cancer. Jupiter in the natal chart indicates the place where we most thrive, grow and learn, but without effort and strain. If it is well placed in the natal chart, one can grow to become a moral, good, honest and compassionate person who is able to teach others and to protect them. Also, it develops a tendency to the large and exciting trips and sporting spirit. It brings money, abundance and prosperity, as well as favoritism in the difficult and scarce moments. It develops the spiritual potential, mercy and goodness. It makes great travelers, philosophers, sages, scholars and spiritual teachers. It develops the idle faith in a better tomorrow. It brings success, satisfaction, money and beautiful things. If it is weak in the natal chart, it creates libertines, gourmets, affair lovers; it wakes the extravagancy, exaggeration, hedonism and immorality. People with the strong Jupiter are often rich, large, successful and satisfied. The well placed Jupiter can enhance or emphasize religiosity. Jupiter in the body governs the hips, liver, gall bladder, pancreas and the upper legs. Some astrologers believe that it is responsible for diabetes and certain groups of tumors. This is possible if at the time of birth it is extremely damaged or a person did not care much about health.

In business astrology Jupiter could talk about the publishing, professorships, politics, diplomacy, sport, big companies and firms, advertising, banking, working abroad, transport, energy, tourism, shipbuilding and seafaring.

Jupiter takes almost twelve years to circle the Zodiac, which means that it stays in one sign for about a year.

Jupiter in mythology: the Roman god Jupiter is identical to the Greek supreme god Zeus. Zeus was the son of Saturn. He became the supreme god when he had removed his father Saturn (Chronos) from the throne. Zeus shared the power with his brothers: Poseidon (Neptune) ruled the seas; Hades ruled the underworld, while he ruled the sky.

Jupiter rules the cycle from fifty-six to sixty-seven years of age.

Astrosymbolism of Jupiter: libraries, the Bible, a lawyer, diplomats, statesmen, doctors, wise men, priests, philanthropists, books, philosophy, travel, distance, money, goods, professor, lectures, goodness, mercy, kindness, optimism, saint, enjoyment, philosophical mind, luxury, morality, justice, globe, passport, religion...

## Saturn

Unlike Jupiter, which is expansive and tends to grow and spread, the planet Saturn has the need for collecting, summarizing, restriction, radical restrictions, retreat and disintegration (demolition, decay, erosion...). When a man is under the strong influence of Saturn, or is in a period when it is dominant in the natal chart, the person learns to travel alone through life with a small bundle on his back, often deprived of help, support and understanding of others. For this reason in the days of Saturn, people often quarrel with their relatives, friends and family, because they are forced to deal with anxiety and problems. Since people usually do not accept this complex and painful lesson, it happens that they lack support even from the most precious beings. Either way, the planet Saturn imposes spiritual progress through great suffering, the loss of loved ones, permanent or temporary isolation. Its lessons make difficult changes, jam, blocking any kind of growth, slowing down every idea or pressure in the field of life that are already poor by birth. However, it sometimes encourages child birth, marriage, family planning or buying a house. However, all this goes with the significant spiritual growth, serious attitude and rigid views on life. Although it is the most beautiful planet (the attention is attracted by its rings) it is difficult to say that people accept it with the welcome and understanding. Saturn faces a man with poverty, transience and all kinds of suffering that he forgets, denies or suppresses in life (illness, death, loss, old age, poverty...). In order to get close to the absolute truth during his lifetime a man is compelled to take the knocks that he believed were always intended only for the others. Saturn often travels with the motto "the wheel of fortune is turning", and we often see that the rich also cry and die, the thief is punished and humiliated, and perhaps some miserable wretch suddenly becomes respected, wealthy and famous. Saturn's lessons are also strong in mundane (collective) astrology, where we see nations rising dramatically, being known as miserable and poor, or they used to buy shoes and cold meat in our stores. Saturn persistently shows that there is a time for everything and everyone, for the ups and downs and through its darkness it reminds a man or people that their time has come.

In its transits, Saturn pays particular attention to the people who make mistakes, hurt, deceive, rob or invest badly. In the days of its domination it shows no compassion, no matter whether in the past we thought that we were beautiful, heavenly, fair and how grabbing someone's money was in fact a useful thing.

Saturn will always punish a sloth and a tyrant, and reward an anguished soul. This implies a renunciation, and awakes the depression in people, pessimism and ascetic approach to life. When it is well placed in the natal chart it brings durability, accuracy, stamina, meticulousness, pettiness, narrow-mindedness, rigor, cold and restrained emotions. It helps people who are patient and eventually brings them peace and stability. Although everything is so, it encourages the processes of aging and decay, and is responsible for the disease, death, each type of disability and deformity (midgets, the poor, and disabled, crippled...). Its transits deposit waste material in the body, promote diseases and awake the tangible fears (envy, jealousy, the feeling of nothingness, and transience). Saturn signifies bones, teeth, hair, and it encourages rheumatism, arthritis, gallstones, bone fractures, loss of hair... Saturn rules the signs of Aquarius and Capricorn, it is strong in Libra, and dangerous (malignant) in the signs of Aries, Cancer and Leo.

Its color is black and all shades of gray, a day of the week is Saturday. It corresponds to blue sapphire, onyx and amethyst. In the East it is called Shani and it is highly respected because it rules the length of life, and how each of us loves to live, we are often at its mercy. If it is good in the natal chart it can develop methodology, principle, routine and responsibility. Its negative aspects are lethargy, depression, stiffness, laziness, hatred and perversity.

Saturn takes almost thirty years to go around the Zodiac.

Saturn in mythology: Chronos (Saturn) castrated his father Uranus and overthrew him from the throne. Later, he was defeated by his son Zeus who threw him into the abyss. It could somehow symbolize the battle between the good and the evil and the eternal desire of a man to grip the matter versus spiritual values.

Saturn in business astrology: mining, geology, history, construction, architecture, forestry, policy, heavy industry, justice, hard physical work, dentistry, agriculture, construction materials, state affairs...

Astrosymbolism of Saturn: nausea, hard work, the poor, the elderly and poor people, black people, grandfather, father, fear, sustainability, disease, deafness, walls, cold, acidic food, skeleton, ambition, materialism, hostility, greed, perversion, seriousness, character, workers, servants, avarice, all the old things, history, fortresses, sadness, tiredness, jealousy, stubbornness, savings, skepticism, repression, mine, worry, shame, slowness, malnutrition, dangerous and insidious animals, obstacles, meticulousness, dedication, accuracy...

# *Saturn in the signs of the Zodiac*

*Saturn in Aries* makes ambition, leads to a bad marriage, or a marriage out of interest, the teeth are weak and brittle, and the hair is thin and often falls out in youth. There is no excessive love for sports, and it can also develop stubbornness and bad deduction. The gift for music and innovation are noticed.

*Saturn in Taurus* develops practical skills, stubbornness, materialism and bad sense of timing. It is particularly important in agriculture and construction. It is bad for singers, but it contributes to artistic affinities.

*Saturn in Gemini* can bring severe mental illnesses or weakness, if it is weakly positioned in the natal chart, and in a better variant it develops intelligence. It poorly affects the operation of nerves and lungs.

*Saturn in Cancer* can cause cancer, tuberculosis, stomach ailments and the heavy character. A special attachment or concern for parents is noticed, a strong memory, patriotism and understanding of traditional values and history. With this position of Saturn, one of the parents suffers severely.

*Saturn in Leo* creates heart problems, pains in the spine, deformity of the spine and flat feet. It is responsible for the strong and bright teeth, and poor and thin hair. It causes the excessive ambition in a man, the emphasized ego and stubbornness. It is responsible for creative and artistic abilities. There is an antagonism between father and grandfather. It is the weak position for the male children, marriage and the father.

*Saturn in Virgo* feels good, and it exerts its quality there through the good organization, methodology, convenience and practical logic. On the other hand, it may present stinginess and excessive attachment to matter, and also the intestinal and stomach problems. Saturn in Virgo develops mental abilities.

*Saturn in Libra* is manifested through relationships and the need to harmonize the relations as much as possible. It develops the just spirit, responsibility and the sense of beauty. It can also symbolize the problems in marriage, provided that the second marriage is somewhat better, skin problems and problems of the urogenital tract. This position of Saturn brings success, victory and the good life abroad.

*Saturn in Scorpio* is manifested through the excessive protection from the outside environment through the self-reliance and values. It can awaken evil whim in a man, an unpleasant character and the need for every kind of control. Its position can cause the disease of the urinary tract or prostate, kidney failure and other severe genital problems.

*Saturn in Sagittarius* is manifested in a visionary way, dynamically and with the tendency to meet various ideals. It is righteous, facing the truth and higher goals. The increased ambition is noticed and a patronizing attitude toward the others. Its weakness is the inability to persevere in its plans, it quickly burns and changes tendencies and aspirations leading to failure or the lack of commitment.

*Saturn in Capricorn* is manifested through the gradual, patient and careful progression with many tactical motives and energy saving. The caution, coldness and cruelty are constantly present, as well as the inability to accept the new trends and patterns. On the other hand, there is a tendency to preserve traditional values, to intensify patriotism and at all costs preserve the family and its legacy. Although it is a sign of Saturn's exaltation it often brings rheumatism, gout, bad teeth and a very strong hair. It brings success in high military and state honors and in some cases a long life.

*Saturn in Aquarius* is manifested through human aspirations and the desire to get people as close as possible to the universal truth by expanding horizons and knowledge. It is capable of accepting new trends and keeping up with the times. Its position in Aquarius can provide good offspring, solid life and healthy sons. Also, it can create a number of hostilities because of sharp and unusual attitudes. There is a strong mental activity (similar to the Saturn in Gemini).

*Saturn in Pisces* manifests itself protectively, cautiously, with the great deal of restraint and reserve which it keeps for itself and rarely shares with others. If Saturn is the ruler of the ascendant, a man can develop artistic inclinations, visions and the overemphasized intuition. There is also a fear, distrust, skepticism and suspicion of everything that others say or in the manner of their operation. On the other hand there is a desire to help people, or at least sympathize with them. Its position in Pisces sometimes creates the mental weakness, irrational fears and false goodness that go along with the hidden and increased ambition.

## *Transcendental planets - Uranus, Neptune and Pluto*

Transcendental planets are the newly discovered planets. The last one discovered was Pluto, which the astronomers deprived of the planet status, and they saw it in 1930. Pluto is certainly still important in astrology. Traditional and Jyotish astrology do not recognize the importance of these planets, which is also rigid and intransigent attitude. On the other hand, Western astrologers have gone much further, and they attributed properties to these planets using psychology and relying too much on the model of Jung's collective unconscious. For this reason, a western astrologer often cannot imagine the year that expects the Natus, whether his destiny is good, whether the Natus (born) will have children and when fractures, success, glory and coronation expect him. In modern astrology, everything is possible, and the horoscope of a man who suffers from paranoid schizophrenia is often interpreted as the reformer's horoscope, a chart of a sick man as a potential guru horoscope or a sportsman and the like. Either way, the transcendental planets are important in the natal, business and mundane astrology. Let's start from the beginning.

# *Uranus*

Uranus is the planet discovered in 1781 by astronomer William Herschel, and insurgency, subversion, eccentricity, originality and unconventionality are attributed to it. Uranus is always against tradition and all that is old, archaic and somehow fixed and boring. It awakens the strong individuality in a man and the ability to be completely his own and different. The same goes for the collective events - the fall of the Bastille, the October Revolution and other revolutions and upheavals. The discovery of the steam locomotive, the development of railways and telegraphs are related to Uranus. Either way, if Uranus is powerful at birth, exalted or heavily aspected, it allows a turbulent and dynamic life, discoveries, sudden changes and movings. Uranus' man is a visionary ready to change and reshape the world trends. Often these are the individuals that others do not accept fully, because we are all afraid of new things and changes. In a bad setting Uranus triggers events which are impossible to be influenced. These are often the dangers of electricity, machinery, explosions, traffic accidents, fires, lightning... Uranus brings out the difficult character in a man and courage that is often not of this world. Uranus cannot bring a lot to a housewife or a doorman, but it is especially important for people who make a living out of their ideas and discoveries, as well as engineers, electricians, astrologers, programmers, spiritualists... Uranus is credited with the awakening of cosmic consciousness in Tesla, Edison and the spiritual teachers who marked the time, and to the mortals in good setting, it brings greater gains and positive life turnovers. It is not desirable that Uranus makes stressful aspects to the personal planets and the ruler of the Zodiac, since it always brings problems, physical or mental suffering. Uranus is the co-ruler of Aquarius, it feels good in the sign of Scorpio, and its weakness is manifested in the sign of Taurus.

Uranus needs eighty-four years to circle the Zodiac (sidereal revolution period) and it has temperature of -210 degrees Celsius. Uranus is not visible with the bare eye.

Uranus in business astrology: cybernetics, physics, nuclear physics, psychology, energy, power, computers, internet, radio appliances, telephones, aviation, inventions, electrical engineering, engineering...

Uranus in mythology: In Greek mythology Uranus was the first master of the world, only to be later unseated from the throne by his son Chronos, cutting his genitals with a sickle.

Astrosymbolism of Uranus: free will, genius, invention, all electrical things, homosexuality, gambling, lottery, originality, perversion, perversity, disobedience, special gifts, engineers, astrology, parapsychology, socialism, awareness, enlightenment, internet, rockets, magic, machines, antennas, innovation, hippies, inspiration, hackers, cosmonauts...

## *Neptune*

Neptune was discovered by Johan Gale in 1846. Neptune was the Roman god of the sea, and it fully corresponds to the Greek Poseidon. Poseidon was given the authority over all waters, aquatic creatures and deities. It signifies the spiritual life, metaphysics, philosophy and it governs all kinds of deception, mental patients, alcoholics, drug addicts, mystics, musicians, talented artists, visionaries, hermits... Each of its contacts with the personal planets makes a unique mark on the character and personality development. When Neptune was discovered, Franz Mesmer in Vienna was dealing with hypnosis, the whole world was infatuated with the ideas about religion and spirituality, and it was the announcement of many hippie movements that later appeared in Europe and America. Neptune rules the feet and its element is water. It governs the sign of Pisces, it is exalted in Aquarius, and it is weak in Leo and Virgo. Under its influence the incredible musicians are formed, mystics and spiritual leaders who can often be severe rogues or self-proclaimed spiritualists. Neptune draws weak and gentle people into problems, so we here often come across drunkards, mollusks, weaklings, drug addicts, sectarians or eccentrics. Neptune brings out the need for concealment in a man, every kind of escape from the reality and real life. It affects poorly the nervous system and self-confidence. It is linked to the insidious diseases which it is impossible to trace or impossible to treat. It is believed to be responsible for the mysterious murders, kidnappings and disappearances of persons, any kind of confusion and secrets that sooner or later draw a man into trouble. It would be good that at birth Neptune makes no conjunction to the ruler of the horoscope or some other stressful aspects with the personal planets (Sun, Moon, Mercury, Venus, and Mars) because its influence is rather suspicious, and sometimes dangerous. Neptune is a very slow planet, and it takes about one hundred and sixty-five years to circle the Zodiac.

Neptune in business astrology: theology, art theory, oceanography, oil, chemicals, pharmaceuticals, perfumes and cosmetics manufacturing, tobacco industry, the production of coffee and tea, places to rest and recover - homes, hotels, the city by the water, rest homes, temples, monasteries, ashrams, spiritual centers, plumbing jobs, certain branches of medicine (pharmacy, psychiatry...), the music industry, the production of beverages that are massively used (Coca-Cola, Pepsi...), film industry (Hollywood), working in saunas or massage centers, fishing, seafaring, shipbuilding...

Astrosymbolism of Neptune: petrol, photos, ideals, homeopathy, spirituality, weakness, fear and deception, vision deception, intuition, meditation, prayer, mental weakness, madness, music, perversion, nymphomania, erotic underwear, water, seas and oceans, religion, pond, sedatives, makeup, utopia, occult, higher states of consciousness, the plants that cause hallucinations, spiritual reading, mask, detective, spy, hijackers, drunkard, intangible things, exaggeration, worship, cameras, inspiration, tea, coffee, chocolate...

# *Pluto*

Pluto was discovered by Clyde Tombo on 02/18/1930, and immediately after this discovery the Third Reich was formed and the whole demonic machinery that created the slaughterhouses, concentration camps and gas chambers. Pluto is the god of the underworld or hell by mythology and it carries within itself demonic powers, perversion, sadism, every kind of brutality, wisdom, and a brilliant mind. If it is well placed it gives great physical energy, a strong spirit, the power to manipulate the masses, it has a negative effect on the psyche, creating magicians, bioenergetics and mental complications. It is linked to the institutions of power, the masonry and people who work "behind the curtain". It wakes up the need for changes in a man that can be quite painful and difficult. It is responsible for many mental illnesses, split personality, or morbid fears. Its influence is quite strange, radical and unforgettable. As if this planet is satisfied only when everything is destroyed, discarded, forgotten, buried, and started afresh. For this reason, it is often credited with widowhood, fatalistic events or tragedies in the family that can never be forgotten. Pluto influences the mass movements or trends. Some astrologers believe that it governs the politics, military sciences, electronics, and global virtual network, underground communication and underground wealth, lasers, superconductors and atomic energy. To the common man it can bring the inheritance, insidious diseases, a strong sexual appetite, danger, the unpleasant and dramatic events, while to the powerful people it brings the enormous wealth, great power and charisma. In contact with the personal planets it can evoke the special propensities, talents and creative potential, but it can never be good for physical and mental health. Pluto is the co-ruler of the sign of Scorpio, and some Russian astrology schools believe that it governs the sign of Aries, which is pretty bad and untested hypothesis. Pluto is the secret of life and death. A man will never accept death as the complete liberation and a new birth, which actually is Pluto - at the expense of someone's ending, there sprouts a new life.

Where someone's end and death is seen, automatically we see that it is a very good chance for someone else.

Pluto in business astrology: military science, criminology, politics, electronics, big business, chemical industry, banking, pawns, weapons, explosives, weapons of mass destruction, surgery, gerontology, pathology, recycling, lasers, energy, heavy industry, information connections, metro, underground construction, ore mining, oil, psychotherapy, hypnosis, computer technology...

Astrosymbolism of Pluto: wizard, extremity, microbiology, kundalini energy, power, hell, catacombs, toxins, magic, hacker, computer virus, rocket fuel, missiles, sadism, perversion, sex, resurrection, volcanos, enigmatic and mysterious people, mines, dumps, septic tank, spies, snake, underground space, nihilism, the brutality, the obsession, danger...

# Astrosymbolism - the Zodiac signs

Astrologers believe that the entire universe is made up of elements that complement each other so that everything works perfectly. Such a perfect functioning of things and interweaving of different events is called the synchronicity. This would mean - what is the macrocosm like, so is a microcosm, what is the cosmic body like, so is the individual body. Thus, the symbolism of the elements interweaves in large and small things. For everything that happens in our little lives and in the world, there are good reasons unfathomable to us, hiding in the finest cosmic games and events.

The belt of eight degrees on either side of the ecliptic is called the Zodiac, and it has a certain vibration and frequency that make people behave differently, differently express their energy, think and live differently. Assessing the quality of the Zodiac signs and the meaning of certain planets found in the particular Zodiac sign, allows the astrologer to understand the character of the born authentically and accurately, and therefore his fate.

(The ecliptic represents the projection of the Earth's orbit around the Sun on the celestial sphere, or the apparent annual path of the Sun).

## *Aries*

Symbolizes all that is young, dynamic, new and animating. It is a masculine, fiery, cardinal sign of the choleric temperament. In Greek mythology it symbolizes Fris, son of King Atmant and Efela. The mother advised Fris to escape on the golden Ram to avoid death from the other Atmant's wife Ino. Fris will later sacrifice his sister in order to be saved. Hence the story of the selfishness of Aries comes. Since this sign symbolizes the beginning of the spring, in astrology it is taken as a good time to start new things. It is under the rule of the planet Mars, which makes these people piercing, self-conscious and courageous. Its color is red, and it is recommended for people who lack self-confidence, initiative and truculence. If someone possesses all of these qualities, it would be good to avoid decorating the interior in this color and wearing red clothing because it can awaken rage, anger and aggression. A disease comes to Aries because they overstrain and overwork themselves and because of strength, which they use in vain in order to compete with stronger or better opponents. They can suffer from diseases of the head, face and blood vessels in the head. The common manifestations are: neuralgia, migraine, problems of red blood cells, insomnia and hair loss. Authorities believe that Aries should eat apples, salads and fish, and avoid strong meat (especially pork). The intake of large amounts of water and chamomile tea is also recommended. Aries at work symbolizes energy, military industry, powerful energy sources, appliances, machine building, metallurgy, technical science, sport, construction and innovation. If there are emphasized elements of Aries in the chart, it is very likely that a person will strive for such operations.

The best period for Aries is the very beginning of spring, and the weakest is the fall. This sign underestimates the difficulties and problems; he wants it all now and immediately and reacts quickly and forcefully. Aries weighs the power, exceeds the limits of his endurance, he likes to compete and try out his force even with the much stronger opponent.

His number is one, and his metal is iron. This part of the Zodiac corresponds to red rocks, diamonds, coral and amethyst. Aries can find strength in nettle, sage and burdock, hawthorn, radish, onion and garlic. If we want to apply the plants' treatment to Aries, we can use carnation.

Aries completely corresponds to the parts of England and France, in particular describes the Germans and Germany, Israel, Poland, Denmark, Syria and Korea. The authorities believe that the following cities also belong to the symbolism of Aries: Birmingham, Verona, Naples, Marseille, Krakow and Florence. Aries corresponds to all sharp and pointed objects, but also symbolizes courage, arrogance, rashness, leaders, warriors and soldiers, open approach towards life, surgeries, injuries, wounds and in some cases a modest intelligence. Aries also symbolizes the sandy, dry and hilly land that is not too shabby.

The symbolism of Aries: the beginning, the new, head, a pioneer, horns, technician, an engineer, a hairdresser, a bricklayer, a blacksmith, welder, hat, inflammation, fire, openness, impetuosity, bravery, headaches, wounds, roof, hot food...

Significant fixed stars of Aries: Deneb Kaitos, Algenib, Alderamin, Alpheratz, Baten Kaitos, Al Ferg, and Vertex.

Significant fixed stars in the constellation of Aries: Sharatan and Hamal.

## *Taurus*

Taurus is related to the thick, fixed energy and energy that can hardly be changed, and such force creates people who are slow or cannot change, they are rigid, hard to accept new things and they need more time to comprehend a life problem. It is a passive female energy whose symbol is the earth. So, this time we have fixed earthy, passive, feminine sign of the melancholic temperament. This part of the Zodiac represents the beauty of spring, childhood, pleasure and every kind of comfort. The desire for the comfortable life, pleasures and peace is overemphasized. Such peace can be sought in the stable things - a steady job, marriage or the life organization. This part of the Zodiac represents pacifism, and does not cause heavy and dark feelings in people. In this area (Taurus) a man can find happiness, joy, fertility, romanticism, the desire to possess and the gift of music. It is the erotic part of the Zodiac so we find that they are good lovers and skilled seducers. The worst part of the year for Taurus can be the late autumn. His day is Friday because it is ruled by the planet Venus, and his true power is found in the number two.

The authorities believe that the diseases of this sign come from the excessive enjoyment, sexual perversions, food and drinks. They often suffer from the illnesses of the neck, the vocal cords, angina, diphtheria, tumors, diabetes, diseases of the trachea and larynx, thyroid, and venereal diseases.

Health can be found in the regular workout, occasional self-restraint and leisured walks. They can also find strength in the homeopathic treatment.

Taurus can be identified in the following occupations: banker, architect (with elements of Capricorn and Libra), natural sciences (botany), agriculture, trade and financial area management, decorative-applied art, design, accessories (handbags and wallets), construction, and building materials (tiles, laminate, wallpaper, carpets...), cooking, cosmetics, and patisserie and jeweler business.

Taurus corresponds to sapphire, emerald and alabaster. His energy is recognized in light blue and pink color, and corresponds to the following plants: flax, olive, lily, rose, violet, spinach, beans, squash... Taurus corresponds to the following cities: Leipzig, Palermo, Turin, Dublin, Lucerne, Nant and Zurich, while his energy also feels, confirms and manifests itself in Asia, South America, Iran, Belarus, Argentina, the Netherlands (which in itself also has the quality of Cancer), Sweden (as amended by the element of the Scorpio), Cyprus, Finland and Ireland.

Taurus symbolizes plains, fertile fields, meadows and fields.

Important fixed stars in the constellation of Taurus are: Aldebaran, Alkion and Prima Hijadum.

Important fixed stars in Taurus: Mirah, Hamal, Shedir, Kapulus, Algol, Misam, Miram, the Pleiades.

## Gemini

Gemini belongs to the variable, air signs which carry inside the dry and warm component (playful, cheerful, approachable, easy in relationships, extroverted, direct, friendly, inconstant, prone to learning and research, able to adopt and accept everything that comes to life...). Under the rule of the planet Mercury.

In Greek mythology, Gemini is presented by the brothers Castor and Pollux (one mortal and the other immortal). Because of their great love, connection and attachment, the supreme god Zeus passed them among the stars. Gemini represents the eternal children, young people, new trends, wit, oratory, intelligence, skill, ability, flexibility and bisexuality. They represent all that is young, charming, clever, little, agile, volatile and subject to influence. This part of the Zodiac (next to Aquarius) is the fastest in thinking, and we often find very clever, intelligent and prudent people among them. For them, it is said that they are thoughtful, less productive, shrewd, skillful, sloppy, dynamic, artists of life, frivolous, profligate, irresponsible and chatty. Their number is three and the day Wednesday. Some believe that their colors are yellow and blue. Looking at the structure and the anatomy of the human body, Gemini takes the area of the upper ribs, parts of the lungs, collarbone, the upper arm, shoulder and shoulder muscles, arms and nerve fibers. The authorities believe that Gemini people suffer as a result of excessive activity and energy dissipation. They often suffer from the nerve weakness, lung diseases (bronchitis and asthma) and the like. Tobacco and coffee should be avoided. At work Gemini people are reflected through the intermediaries, commerce, brokerage, organizational technology, transport, journalism, publishing, painting, literature, and medicine (psychotherapy, psychiatry, neuropathology...).

If we are interested in cities and regions, Gemini corresponds to the following areas: San Francisco, Rio de Janeiro, London, Melbourne, Nuremberg, Brussels, United States, and Lombardy in Italy, Sardinia, Egypt and Nigeria. Gemini symbolizes high places.

The symbolism of Gemini: books, excursions, neighbors, relatives, means of transport, libraries and bookstores, a messenger, a writer, a postman, a passenger, versatility, curiosity, students and teachers, schools, courses, things that are small and functional.

# *Cancer*

Cancer is the fourth sign of the Zodiac, and by its nature it is passive, slow, of the phlegmatic temperament. This space can symbolize the intuition, desire and the need for protection, loyalty, strong patriotism that often goes to the extreme, the need to build a home, a family and cherish the old traditional values that are the legacy of the ancestors. Cancer is ruled by the Moon and its symbol is water, it corresponds to the number four and its day is Monday. Cancer is the most energetic in the summer months, and languishes most when the planets are in Capricorn and Aquarius (at the end of the year). If we look at human anatomy, Cancer rules the stomach and pulmonary part of the body, due to the flood of feelings often suffers from serious diseases (cancer), but is also susceptible to stomach ailments and mental problems. Its colors are white, light blue and silver. Cancer's energy is recognized and reflected in the following stones: quartz, opal, crystal and pearl. The following countries and cities also correspond to it: Venice, Milan, Geneva, Manchester, Amsterdam, Bern, Istanbul, Genoa, Stockholm, and New York, as well as Scotland, the Netherlands, Tunisia, Algeria, parts of Africa.

After the configuration of the terrain, Cancer corresponds to the wet or swampy soils; it also represents springs, ponds and lakes.

Important fixed stars in the constellation of Cancer: Praesepe, Asellus Borealis, Asellus Australis, Acubens.

Important fixed stars in the sign of Cancer: Dirah, Sirius, Castor, Pollux, Procyon...

Symbolism of Cancer's energy is reflected and recognized in the following words: mother, family, roots, genetics, history, personal satisfaction, peace and tranquility, a flashback, intuition, the occult, water surfaces, strong emotions, house and garden, personal property, the most intimate parts of the soul, sensitivity, vegetables, poppy, clover, cucumber, squash, bees and other insects, crabs and oysters.

# *Leo*

Leo is the fifth sign of the Zodiac, and by its nature it is male, fixed, active and choleric. It is under the rule of the Sun, and its symbol is fire. In mythology Leo is linked to Hercules who strangled the Nemean lion in the cave, by approaching him from behind while he was unprepared. This is a story about the treacherous enemies and those who stalk large and special people in order to thwart them, to harm them or stop them from progression. It is believed that this part of the Zodiac is special in everything and that it is bathed in the glare and ability of a man to shine and rise above the dust. According to some, a Leo is allegedly given the task in this life to show the beauty of the Supreme creation, provided that he doesn't forget that creation is not his, but God's. It is also believed that a Leo, after the expressed understanding for the others, receives great presents and gifts of life. A Leo is forever in search of joy, dance, fame and recognition. His energy is warm, spontaneous and full of enthusiasm and cheerfulness. The most fruitful period for a Leo is the period of the summer months, when the Sun is strongest and warmest. A Leo responds to the number five and the last day of the week. His energy is reflected in ruby, gold and diamonds and Western astrologers ascribe the following colors to him: gold, red, orange and yellow. All feline animals suit him. Energy of Leo is recognized in the following plants: palm tree, rosemary, mint, chamomile, lemon, orange, wheat, parsley, cinnamon, laurel and others. If in someone's horoscope there is the overemphasized element of Leo, he/she needs to look for and try luck in the following countries and cities: Prague, Rome, Linz, Madrid, Mumbai, Philadelphia, Chicago, parts of France, Cuba, Florida, Italy (especially Sicily and southern Italy), Peru, Hawaii, Iraq, parts of Romania, the Czech Republic and California. A Leo also corresponds to the following body parts: the main arteries, heart, back and spine. A Leo is quite vital and suffers from angina and other heart diseases. He is able to be treated by the autosuggestion and quickly recovers after the life crises and shipwrecks.

According to the configuration of the terrain Leo corresponds to the joyful, bright and lively places that are often featured, forested and mountainous terrains and partly jungles and deserts.

Energy of Leo is fully compliant with these words: children, father, power, manager, boss, authority, leader, king, emperor, actor, theater, creativity, organizer, politician, great figure, stage, supervisor, optimism, courage, generosity, pomposity and excessive self-love.

Important stars in the constellation of Leo: Regulus, Zosma and Denebola.

Important fixed stars in the sign of Leo: Praesepe, Asellus Borealis, Regulus...

## *Virgo*

Virgo is the sixth sign of the Zodiac, which includes passive, feminine energy, of the variable quality and melancholic temperament. It is an earthy (financial and practical) sign ruled by the planet Mercury. Observing the anatomy of the human body, we can say that Virgo rules the abdomen, stomach, pancreas and intestines. During lifetime, they suffer from insomnia, stomach problems, nerve diseases... Their diseases come from life composed of unnecessary details, worries and all kinds of observations that cannot strengthen the character, nor create a solid spirit. For this reason, in time they convert to harridans, people prone to sarcasm, cynicism, and bitter observations. They are rarely able to be spontaneous, happy and optimistic, and flaws like avarice, austerity and pessimistic character are attributed to them by some astrologers. In mythology Virgo is linked to Demeter, the goddess of Earth and agriculture who had a daughter Persephone (today it is often observed that the emphasized Virgo in the horoscope gives a strange, unbreakable and unhealthy relationship with mother). Demeter had the need to keep her daughter beside her forever, but Hades (God of Hell) foiled her plan and took her to him. The myth goes further so that Persephone spends half the year with her mother (in the spring) and half the year with Hades (God of Hell). This is, of course, the story of the strange and possessive parents who do not allow their children to become independent, to grow up and find themselves a partner. Either way, a Virgo does not enjoy a good reputation due to poignancy, lack of enthusiasm, optimism and lack of bright ideas. However, no one can dispute the knowledge they gain on the road of life, and the responsibility that repairs everything of the above mentioned. If there is an emphasized element of Virgo in the horoscope, a person should be able to seek happiness in the following countries and cities: parts of Poland, Switzerland, Brazil, and parts of India, Turkey, Greece and its islands, Egypt, Uruguay, Los Angeles, Athens, Paris, Basel, Lyon, Boston, Toulouse, New Orleans, Moscow and Strasbourg. Energy and quality of Virgo can be completely found in the following words: meticulous, analytical skills, discipline, order, diligence, knowledge, practicality, prudence, restraint, dullness, poverty, humble living conditions, alienation, shyness, anxiety, drugs, medicine, illness, small animals, routine, reliability, small stuff, cheap and useful items, secretarial work, accountant, associate, assistant, servant, accuracy, craftsmen, artisans and others.

Virgo represents wheat and corn fields, plains, beaches and terrains that are at the sea level.

Important stars in the constellation of Virgo: Zaviava, Zani, Vindemiatrix, Kafir, Spike, Kambalia.

Important fixed stars in the sign of Virgo: Zosma, Cox, Denebola, Zaviava, Markeb...

## *Libra*

Libra represents the seventh sign of the Zodiac and is ruled by the planet Venus. We are talking about the cardinal, active, masculine sign that is of the sanguine temperament. The first association with the sign of Libra is beauty, elegance, manners, courtesy, and sense of order, harmony and justice. However, in practice it looks a bit different, and we often find Libra people who are desperately begging for love and constantly looking for attention, delights, socializing, because it is impossible to propitiate them to be alone sometimes. They mostly enter into all kinds of relationships that often do not have happy endings. Libra people are related to the urinary tract, kidneys and reproductive organs (along with Scorpio). There is a belief that those born in the sign of Libra have sensitive skin and blood vessels and during their lifetime they often suffer from diabetes and inflammation of the urogenital organs. A Libra can be broken by difficult and unhealthy living conditions, stress, and exposure to hard, physical work. They cannot bear painful family scenes, violence and situations which demand to make decisions, lead and work actively. For this reason, they often make covenants (marriage, partnerships...) in which they feel snug and lulled, and may shift the burden of responsibility onto the others. Because of the unbalanced emotions they can significantly compromise their health. There is also a belief that candies, coffee and salt make a bad influence on them. Libra people recover quickly if they receive the adequate care and attention or spend time walking and resting. No one can deny their good behavior, fine manners, a sense of beauty and talent. The best periods for a Libra are the ninth and tenth month, and the weakest in the spring when the fast planets are placed in the sign of Aries. Libra people are excellent as musicians, photographers, set designers, actors, models and public figures. The same applies to persons who in their horoscope have many planets in the sign of Libra. Their number is seven, a day Friday. Indian astrologers believe that Libras are colorful and white, while Western astrologers believe that they are all shades of blue, green and pink color. Libra corresponds to diamonds, blue sapphire, emerald and white marble. If we look at animals and plants Libra is recognized in the following terms: nightingale, dove, swan, deer, llama, cat, rose, violet, cereals, palm, ash and others. Libra feels great in the following countries and cities: Austria, Argentina, Egypt, Libya, Tibet, China, Peru, Guatemala, parts of Italy (Tuscany), parts of France (Alsace), Vienna, Copenhagen, Lisbon, and Miami, Frankfurt, Johannesburg and others.

Energy of Libra dominates in the following terms: harmony, conformity, beauty, art, music, subtle feelings, pacifism, the need for harmonious relations, publicity, musical instruments, jewelry, boutique, bedroom, painter, artist, actor (with a touch of Leo), gallery, wardrobe, underwear, decorative art objects, the Parliament, etc.

Important fixed stars in the constellation of Libra: Kifa Kifa Borealis and Australis.

Important fixed stars in the sign of Libra: Vindemiatrix, Spica and Arcturus.

## Scorpio

Scorpio is a passive, feminine Zodiac sign of the phlegmatic temperament. Its element is water, but here we can speak of boiling water, which is very different from the other water signs (Cancer and Pisces). Scorpio is ruled by the planet Mars. Modern astrologers believe that it is akin to Pluto, which has recently lost its status of a planet. In mythology it is associated with the hunter Orion, who was punished by the cruel gods for his violent behavior, by sending a small scorpion to kill him. From the mythological story we realize that there is a huge intensity in that Zodiacal band in which the following intertwine: magnetism, mystique, the intellect of every kind, lust, jealousy, twisted and unnecessary hatred and the ability to tackle the immense depth, if a man is searching for the truth and the divine. Life of a Scorpio is always stressful, full of battles, skirmishes and re-climbing, nothing is easy for him but he sees it as a charm. He is loved or rejected, depending on the life cycles and rhythms. It governs the genitals, and often suffers from the sexually transmitted infections, prostate disease, hemorrhoids, colon and hernia. Some think that a Scorpio can digest all, cook and break it down within, and allegedly does not require special care and diet. It is also able to be treated by the suggestion or autosuggestion. The number is eight, and the day Tuesday. It is identified in all shades of red. His qualities are clearly evident in these animals and plants: scorpion, eagle, condor, wolf, dark insects, vultures, wild boar, snake, beetroot, garlic, tobacco, cactus, chili peppers, ivy and others.

Scorpio feels good and copes well in the following countries and cities: parts of Spain (Catalonia and the central part), Algeria, North America, parts of Germany (Bavaria), Scandinavia (especially Norway), parts of Asia, Indochina, Malaysia, Brazil, Bolivia, Morocco, Syria, Korea, parts of the US (Nevada, Montana and others), Jordan, the Philippines, Munich, Dover, Liverpool, Valencia, Washington, New Orleans, Tokyo, Padova...

Scorpio represents cemeteries, dark places, sewers, basements, underground passages, tunnels, ditch, swamp, quicksand, sewerage, waste, places of the lurking danger, catacombs, rivers...

The symbolism of Scorpio completely lives in the following terms: intensity, death, sexuality, testament, inheritance, surgery, wound, jealousy, hatred, fatal connections, adverse events, executors, crime, wealth, occultism, regeneration, and life after death, and passion for life, fight, war, surgeons, powerful people, doctors, diabolic, fear and others.

Important fixed stars in the constellation of Scorpio: Izidis, Akrab, Lesat, Antares, Saul, Acumen...

Important fixed stars in the sign of Scorpio: Princeps, Sirma, Kambalia, Mimoza, Akruks, Kifa Australis, Kifa Borealis, Unukalhai, Agena, Bungula...

## Sagittarius

Sagittarius is the ninth sign of the Zodiac which is ruled by the planet Jupiter. We are talking here about an active, fiery, variable, masculine sign of the choleric temperament. In mythology Sagittarius represents the centaur Chiron, in the upper part of his body bearing the human form, and in the lower part of the body the animal form. Unlike the other centaurs that rampaged and inflicted damage, Chiron helped, healed and taught others. Supposedly Chiron taught Achilles, Castor, Pollux and other heroes. On one occasion he was wounded by a poisoned arrow. Due to the fact that he was immortal, the wound inflicted the terrible pain upon him, and he asked Zeus (the supreme God) to send him to the Lower World (with the other mortals) in order to stop his suffering. Here we can also talk about the "Achilles' heel" carried by each Sagittarius, his physical vulnerability and desire to help others. For this reason, Sagittarius is most worthy of divine grace, because its desires and thoughts are often pure and harmless. A Sagittarius loves life, socializing, traveling, enjoying the pleasures of life, and we can rightfully claim that he often lives the best. This part of the Zodiac is adorned with generosity and the idealistic approach to life. Although youthfulness and lightness are attributed to people who have the emphasized Gemini, the youth and enthusiasm can often be attached to Sagittarius because of the cheerful spirit, and his outlook goes far beyond the physical frame. Sagittarius governs buttocks and thighs, and in life can suffer from various weaknesses, depending on the rest of the horoscope. Apparently sport helps him, recreational walks and spending time outdoors help him, as well. Sagittarius is found in many professions: philosophy, sport, education, politics, acting, public work... His number is nine, the day Thursday, and the following colors are related to him: all shades of blue, turquoise and purple. The following stones heal and help him: turquoise, amethyst and emerald. In the symbolism of Sagittarius, there are the following countries and cities: parts of France (Provence and Burgundy), Hungary (with elements of Fish), Spain (with elements of the Scorpion), Madagascar, Vatican, Romania, Thailand, parts of the United States (Pennsylvania, Ohio, Indiana, Mississippi...), Cologne, Stuttgart, Budapest, Toronto... Sagittarius fully lives in the following terms: width, optimism, cheerfulness, positive spirit, enthusiasm, courage, philanthropist, philosophy, morality, justice, distant travels, foreign countries, publishing houses, religion, professor, teacher, priest, benefactor, generosity, boundless faith and hope, nobility, high goals and ideals, the good...

Sagittarius represents hills, high places, open and clearly visible places.

Important fixed stars in the constellation of Sagittarius: Polis, Spiculum, Facies, Pelagus, ASCE, Manubrium...

Important fixed stars in the sign of Sagittarius: Antares and Rastaban.

## *Capricorn*

Capricorn represents the tenth sign of the Zodiac. It is a feminine, cardinal, passive sign of the melancholic temperament. The symbol of Capricorn is the earth, and therefore, there is a too strong attachment to the matter. Moto of a Capricorn is "I have and I possess", which tells of a great ambition and desire to rise. Capricorn is in mythology represented by the god Ea, the protector of reason and water. For this reason, the Capricorn's upper body is presented in the form of an animal, and the lower part of the body in the form of a siren, which should be associated with sensuality, strong, ground eroticism and animal passion. Because of the mythological story it often happens that people born under this sign or with many planets in Capricorn, enjoy sex without developing special closeness with the partner. Astrologers believe that Capricorn is, because of its ruler Saturn, stingy, cold, often in a bad mood, weak and lukewarm emotions, which may not be completely accurate. The lack of romance, the despotic behavior, restraint and innate skepticism are attributed to them. Apparently, they suffer from various complexes, but are able to live an ascetic life, if they mark the sufficiently clear target. Capricorn spends his time in the best way; he is patient and knows that every being on the planet has its "five minutes". For this reason he works systematically, does not overwork himself like Aries and does not burn unless it is necessary. Although everything is like this, a Capricorn is a good worker, reliable, accurate and responsible. Some astrologers believe that he succeeds later in life, when many disposed of their spears or simply do not see the purpose in what they do. This part of the Zodiac is quite slow, so if there is the emphasized Capricorn in the horoscope (stellium of planets, Ascendant or the Sun in Capricorn) we should not expect the entertainer or the excessively cheerful person, but restrained, hard-working and closed personality. A Capricorn feels safe when he makes money or builds a high fence walls, which should compensate for the fears and make him forget about the mortality and transience of life. Capricorn rules the bones, knees and the complete skeletal system. His number is ten, a day Saturday. It corresponds to all shady colors, but his metal is the lead that symbolizes weight and lack of generosity and pleasure. Capricorn is recognized in tourmaline, onyx (rocks), coal, pitch and the magnet which make this sign especially occult. Energy of the Capricorn is perfectly identified in the following countries and cities: Afghanistan, Bolivia, India, Mexico, Kyrgyzstan, Uzbekistan, a large part of Russia, Bulgaria, Georgia, Iran, New Delhi, Mexico City, Oxford, Novgorod (Gorky) and others.

The symbolism of Capricorn can be recognized in the following terms and concepts: the cold, restraint, calculated behavior, famine, poverty, misery, hardship, remote and poor places, underground passages, catacombs, caves, monuments, stone, bricks, walls, concrete, elephant, rhino, giraffe, goat, the judge, politician, ambitious man, a serious illness, used and old things, reliability, history, distant memories, flashbacks, routines and duties, architect, builder and others.

Capricorn responds to the smelly places, dark spaces, old and rural areas, the high places that are impossible or difficult to reach, caves, rocks and rocky areas.

Important fixed stars in the constellation of Capricorn: Dabih, Oculus, Bos, Armus, Dorsum, Castro, Deneb Algedi...

Important fixed stars in the sign of Capricorn: Spikulum, Polis, Kaus Medius, Facies, Pelagus, ASCE, Manubrium, Vega, Deneb, Peacock, Terebelum...

## *Aquarius*

Aquarius represents the eleventh sign of the Zodiac ruled by the planet Saturn. Some prefer to attribute the rule over Aquarius to Uranus, because those people need to think of themselves as the eccentric, original and attribute to themselves all kinds of other qualities that we find in distinct individuals. So, it is active, air, masculine and fixed sign of the sanguine temperament. If we think about it, Aquarius and Pisces are the least known of all the Zodiac signs. Because of this ignorance we attribute them to the rebellious (James Dean, who was nervous and unmanageable) and we can often read that they tend to every kind of the extreme, but it may not be true. The greatest weaknesses of Aquarius are the partnerships because of their coldness and the inability to easily approach the person they truly love or the most precious one. For this reason they are often alone, divorced or in some special kinds of relationships that often have no future and legality. On the other hand they perfectly fit into society, they are wonderful friends, ready to step in, help and fight for a better tomorrow. In mythology Aquarius is linked to Deucalion, the son of the king of Thessaly, who managed to save himself from the flood in the barge. It should symbolize people who are far ahead of their time - the reformers, or people of the new civilizations. Aquarius is a kind of modern Prometheus who should bring some change and something new to the human kind, but in order to be sacrificed at the end. Thus, the Aquarians are trying to do well to all at their own expense and to the detriment of the person beside them. Aquarius in the Zodiac is the typical human sign - represented by a man with a jug from which water flows and it has much deeper meaning than it is assumed at first. Aquarius suffers from the heart disease, legs, circulation and nerves. The weakest periods for an Aquarius are the summer months, and he feels best at the beginning of the year.

His number is eleven, and the day Saturday. They best correspond to blue, black and turquoise color, as well as the metals lead and aluminum. Aquarius corresponds to the following minerals and precious stones: sapphire, aquamarine, amethyst and magnet. Some believe that Aquarius governs the following plants: willow, birch, cypress, myrtle and rosemary. The following cities and states are under its rule: Salzburg, St. Petersburg, Moscow (with the elements of Taurus), Hamburg, Bremen, Strasbourg, Arizona, Michigan, former Prussia (now Germany), and Russia, Poland, Sweden and others. If we consider the relief and the configuration of the terrain, Aquarius represents the prairie, places where the strong winds blow, hills and plateau.

Aquarius can be found in the following expressions and words: scientist, inventor, technician, internet, electricity, electronics, computer, social networking, X-ray, pilot, inventor, reforms, humanity, an expert on missiles and atomic energy, rebel, contrarian, loner, altruism...

Important fixed stars in the constellation of Aquarius: Sadalsuud, Sadalmelik, Skat.

Important fixed stars in the sign of Aquarius: Dorsum, Sadalsud, Deneb Algedi...

## *Pisces*

They represent the twelfth sign of the Zodiac. It is a variable, water, passive sign of the phlegmatic temperament, ruled by the planet Jupiter. There is a belief that the people born under this sign are strongly affected by the planet Neptune, but still one shouldn't rely much on its influence. In mythology Pisces are associated with Derceto who jumped into the sea to avoid the real life on Earth. Supposedly because of that, the sea god Poseidon punished her by transforming her into a mermaid - half woman and half fish. From this mythological story we can guess how huge is their need for escaping from reality, or hiding from the real life and the suffering imposed by birth. For this reason, Pisces are attributed the divine qualities: mystique, empathy, musicality, ability to contact with the higher beings, closeness to the people, the desire to serve and satisfy, forgiveness and understanding of human weaknesses. However, real life is somewhat different. Some interesting research has shown that Pisces more often strive to the problem than establish a spiritual unity with the people and the gods. For this reason we often notice that the others rescue them from the troubles in which they were involved.

Pisces rule the feet and it is also believed that their psyche is too sensitive, so they isolate themselves and withdraw from people. We find them in all possible professions, which dispute the claim that they are clumsy, impractical and exclusively talented for music. Pisces are the most sensitive in the fall. Astrologers believe that akin to them are the people born in the signs of Taurus, Cancer, Scorpio and Capricorn, which in practice may not be true.

Their number is twelve and the day Thursday. Blue and turquoise colors match them, which indicates the spiritual values, infinity and internal security.

Pisces correspond to the seas, underwater vasts and extremely high places where a man cannot dwell.

Countries and capitals in Pisces: Uruguay, Panama, Portugal, parts of Russia and parts of Hungary, North Africa, Egypt, Florida, New Zealand, Polynesia, parts of the Amazon, Mediterranean, Warsaw, Seville, Venice, Alexandria, St. Petersburg, Jerusalem, Copenhagen, etc.

Pisces are recognized in the following terms: spirituality, sensitivity, intuition, deceit, betrayal, sea, ocean, aquarium, alcoholic, problem, intrigue, secrets, art, photography, remote spots, monastery, narcotics, cigarettes, meditation, chemistry, Hollywood, space, shoes, socks, insane asylums, hospitals, theft, diver, perfumes...

Important fixed stars in the constellation of Pisces: Alrisha and Al Ferg.

Important fixed stars in the sign of Pisces: Sadalmelik, Formalhaut, Deneb Adige, Skat, Situla, Arhernar, Sheat...

# LOVE AND SEXUALITY
## - THE ZODIAC SIGNS

Sexuality is the most sensitive area of human life and a precondition for a good and high-quality relationship or marriage. A human is extremely shy and does not live a real part of his nature, rarely being honest with himself or the partner. Sexual energy is closely connected with money, health and driving power. In order to love someone and enjoy that love, it is necessary to know the needs of your partner. Each Zodiac sign has some sexual and romantic preferences depending on the energy, so the energy of a Virgo is quite different from the needs of a Scorpio. You should cherish your love and sexuality, do not block and suppress it, because everything that is suppressed is fed by the same act.

## *Aries - love and sexuality*

This sign is often overhyped, so people expect them to be passionate, energetic and uncompromising, both in love and sex. Practice has shown that Aries is brilliant at work and a bit weaker in the love field. The truth is that they have a lot of energy, but they are not skilled tacticians, or they are famous for seducing with the scented candles and the ambient music. If you want to seduce them, it is necessary to be open, direct and original. Aries loves contest and competition in bed, so it wouldn't be the best solution to compete with him. It is well known that this sign enjoys violent and the unexpected sex which does not necessarily last long. Their strength lies in the fact that they clearly show what they want and it is easy to get in touch with them and engage into an adventure. They behave strangely in the company of the rivals and competitors, demonstrating a children's kind of jealousy and aggression. Since they burn out in all segments of life, it may occur that later in life they become practically useless

in bed. Aries are not inclined to the atypical sexual preferences, which place them among people who enjoy healthy
sexuality. Both in marriage and in love they develop the
despotic nature which can become a problem if a partner also has a strong personality. They gladly engage in
sexual relationships with people who are equally durable
and willing to experiment. However, such ties seldom lead
to marriage. Aries is often criticized, apart from the passion in bed, for showing a strange coldness, egoism and
selfishness in love. They are also criticized for the lack of
romance, new ideas and empathy. Although loyal in love,
they can hardly understand someone's weakness, volatility or instability. They take what they need, both in bed
and out of it, and because of that they experience serious
emotional crises. If it is a female Aries, it would be advisable for her to choose an effeminate partner who would
be able to compensate for the tenderness. Aries are capable and willing to fight for love and if they want someone,
they will use all their energy to win them over or seduce
them. They are also known for simplifying everything in
love and sex that was initially interesting, and later that
would be treated as a problem or coldness in the relationship. They are rarely inclined to sexual perversions; therefore, they should not be tempted by unusual ideas. Some
old school astrologers believe that they correspond well to
the people born in the sign of Leo, Sagittarius and Libra,
which proved to be the unreliable statement in practice. It
should be mentioned that the famous Casanova was born
in the sign of Aries; he had the urge to seduce thousands
of women. Unfortunately, he was not considered to be a
person who brought happiness in love to the others.

If Aries is particularly emphasized in the female horoscope, it happens that it produces an impulsive, uncompromising, rough and affective woman who falls into conflict situations that often end in physical or verbal confrontations. In some cases, this sign can develop a line
of sadism, especially if Mars is particularly weak in the
horoscope (Cancer, Taurus...), or placed in the weak houses of the horoscope or building the discordant aspects to

the Moon, Uranus and Pluto. Afflictions to Neptune will rarely create ruffians or thugs. Aries cannot boast to be particularly happy in marriage, so he is inclined to flirting and adventures. In particular, the effect of his sexuality is especially diminished if Aries is the exiting sign (the ascendant), while Mars is in Virgo, Cancer or Pisces. In these cases a sexual indifference can occur, a lack of desire and even the impotence in the midlife.

> *Note: If we talk about Aries, then we think of the Sun in Aries, the ascendant in Aries, the ruler of the ascendant in Aries, or stellium (more planets in Aries). The students of astrology shouldn't derive complete conclusions about the character or sexuality of a person, length of marriage, or quality of life, based on the certain factors and without taking into account the rest of the horoscope. Because of the simplifying and banalizing astrology, it happens that many people study astrology, and yet there are few real astrologers. The same happens in singing or any other business. Many people sing, but the real nightingales are really scarce and rare.*

## *Taurus - love and sexuality*

There is a belief in astrology that Taurus is slow, sluggish and inert, which is not far from the truth, but there is also a belief that they are clumsy, sleepy and lazy in love, which is certainly not true. This sign governs pleasures, inappropriate satisfactions and every kind of exaggeration. Their feelings are lasting and stable, they do not experience major crises, and can love long and well. They are particularly attracted by Leo, and the traditional astrologers believe they get along best with those in the sign of Scorpio. The truth is that they cannot experience a complete harmony with any of these two signs. Unlike Aries, this sign is capable of atypical and strange sexual relationships. Some parts of the sign are especially problematic, and it is believed that the first half of the Taurus is particularly happy. Taurus is good for long-lasting relationships and marriages that can be permanent and stable. They are capable of providing safety, comfort and convenience. They are able to endure a nervous, choleric and aggressive partner, the victim of hormones and all kinds of inner changes. They can be possessive, although at first glance it does not seem so. They don't like monotony, routine and the everyday life, so you need to invest a lot of energy in order to make them happy in love and sex. Since Taurus is one of the most sensual signs, and it is hard for them to function with someone who doesn't have high sexual needs or can live in celibacy. Taurus is particularly beautiful, sensuous with the sensual lips. Women are often plump, rounded and fertile. If you are in love with them, you should not be surprised if they cannot understand you or are not capable to change. Taurus thinks slowly and such inertia may surprise or offend the partner. For this reason the deep, philosophical conversations that should strengthen or deepen the relationship, are not recommended. You can often surprise them with a gift and practical things that are real aphrodisiac. Sometimes love comes up over the stomach, and do not be surprised if before sex you go to a good lunch. If you want to get more intense and deeper connection, you should first create a sense of comfort. Taurus does not enjoy poverty, social scenes and indigence. Taurus rejoices in the abundance and prosperity, and it is important that the partner is well-situated, or to instill at least some kind of safety. This of course is not necessary, but one day it can become a problem when the passion wanes. Taurus people are considered to be the unimaginative lovers, which is completely untrue. They have large reserves of energy and often know how to pleasantly surprise the partner in bed. They enjoy fun, good company, food and drink. Although everything is so, it is frequent that people in this sign suffer from sexual frustrations and limitations that they cannot live in everyday life. It is rarely mentioned that a certain part of this sign is especially perverse. This is particularly the case when there is a conjunction of Mars and Venus in that sign.

# Gemini - love and sexuality

Gemini cannot brag about being deep, intense and too serious in romantic relationships, therefore they are causing headaches to the others. In their volatility there is often no shred of malice, so they are often forgiven for being late for a meeting or for having not fulfilled a promise. Some astrologers persistently claim that Gemini people like to communicate, so people think they are asexual, curious and superficial. It seems that they just want to chat, socialize, play and meet people, which is completely untrue. Gemini people think a lot about love and sex, love to experiment and engage in bold love risks and ventures. It is true that the conversation is essential to them as well as every kind of communication. They like to make conversations which stimulate or arouse their sexual desire. They also like to hear about experiences, but that does not mean they are not possessive, so you needn't tell them spicy stuff from the past at all costs. They tolerate painful scenes, break-ups, the fact that they are not loved or deceits more easily. Because they often cheat too, impermanent and flexible as they are, they are never bored. If you engage in a sexual or romantic relationship with them, you should know that there will be much adrenaline and turmoil abound. Fidelity is not a strong point of this sign, so there is the need for flirting, and the relationship must always be fresh, young and diverse. What Gemini is amused by in sex at this moment, at the next is falling into oblivion. They gladly try out things in bed which much bolder people would not dare to venture. They can hardly function with people who are closed, silent, introverted, without curiosity and uninspiring. They can hardly bear possessive and devoted relationships which take place in the four walls, far from the sight of others. Gemini people love pastime, and if in the horoscope there is no water or earth element emphasized, they will go through life like children, forever in search of pleasures and new experiences. People born in the sign of Gemini are accused of being cold in love, of satisfying only their own needs and of not having much understanding for their partners. As they are the victims of thoughtful processes, trapped in their own bodies, burdened with many questions and the uncertainties, they frequently establish relationships and marriages full of mystery, ambiguity and complicated situations. Because of the double life and the emotional volatility, it would be best for them to choose partners who are not mentally slow and dull. If you are entertaining, original and ready to always bring something new into life, the relationship with them would be rich, quality and meaningful. It is believed that Gemini fits well in love with the air and fire signs. There is also a belief that they cannot achieve a quality relationship with people born in the signs of Pisces and Scorpio.

## Cancer - love and sexuality

Ever since the old times it is believed that Cancers are made for home atmosphere only, and that they solely dream to weed a little garden around a farm and plant roses in the garden. There is also a belief that only the fiery signs enjoy strong passions, while others are far behind them. The interesting thing is that the majority of examinees insisted that the best lovers in their lives were in the sign of Cancer and that they experienced the most intense passions with the members of this sign. Even the famous Joan Collins in her memoirs claimed that her best and most intense experience was with a man born in the sign of Cancer. Either way, this part of the Zodiac is particularly susceptible to enjoyments, sexual experiences and love pleasures. In addition to the great commitment, need for bonding and strong emotions, Cancer possesses exceptional stamina and in a few cases while working with private clients I learned that Cancers are not satisfied with the quick sex and rarely "ignore these actions". What Cancer owns, unlike the other signs, is a compound of emotion and passion, especially trying to satisfy the partner, they are not selfish and cold as can sometimes be the case with the air and fire signs. This is especially true for men, and if they happen to have both the strength and the endurance, all this goes combined with the need to make the other one enjoy in bed. For this reason women are often satisfied because they do not feel the emptiness and selfishness offered by the other men. On the other hand, Cancers are tremendously possessive which can be an aphrodisiac at one point (partner feels good because he feels desirable), and on the other hand, it creates unnecessary debates, distressing scenes, and in extreme cases even hatred and rough emotions. Cancers have a sick need to appropriate everything and strongly attach to people, so they usurp everything that comes into their life. For this reason they are often good and loyal in marriages and romantic relationships, but they can be extremely annoying, ready for painful discussions, ascertaining of guilt and accusations that the partner is cold or undedicated. Men are leading in this particular thing and in time they may turn into real "housewives" ready for the determination of partner's guilt. It is true that Cancers are very deep, emotional, and receptive and enjoy being loved or that someone pays attention to them. They give a lot in bed and in cohabitation, and on the other hand they require much in return, which is a great challenge and a burden. If they imagine that they are unloved, the relationship can turn into a real torture, and the days are filled with difficult situations. Cancers often fantasize to build family with their partners, have children, and eventually have the need to stay indoors most of the time and spend it in an intimate setting or at home. They are rarely prosaic or simple. They carefully measure how much they are given and given in return, and they also love to provide security and protection. They need to feel strong and if the partners cause negative emotions or restlessness, it happens that they completely fail in bed.

## Leo - love and sexuality

In astrological texts we often find that Leos are good parents, loyal, faithful and loyal in marriages, which is somewhat true. On the other hand, it is rarely written about the fact that they are pretty miserable in love, whether they have been seriously hurt emotionally, or they have injured the partner or the loved one. Leo has an urgent need for somebody to love and respect them, but in their universe there is no place for others, so the people are forced to abandon their friends and loved ones in order to maintain the harmony of love. The problem is that this part of the Zodiac (Leo) has no expressed awareness of others, and they often find that they are not getting enough or that their love and attention were denied to them in a strange way. Leo has a huge amount of energy, enthusiasm and life passion which must certainly be reflected in bed. The desire to prove them is quite strong, and they make a lot of effort to leave a good impression in the marriage bed and out of it. Leo loves flirting, seduction, beautiful people, glamour, so they do not prefer making love on the grass or in the neighbor's barn in order to popularize rural tourism. Here it is about the people who respect themselves enough to think they deserve a lot of life. They seek continual admiration and adoration from their partners which can become a real burden in time. If you love a Leo it is best not to talk about his weaknesses because you can hurt, embarrass and undermine his confidence. Sometimes it is necessary to pay him a tribute or say things that warm his soul and his shimmering ego. Leos are trying hard to enlighten somebody with love; they are often generous and try to overshadow their predecessors by their endurance, strength and passion. On the other hand, they do not realize that others do not have enough energy to compete with them, regardless of whether it is about sex or other life activities. Leo's jealousy is somewhat less emphasized than at the water signs, and the pre-marital relationships are quite rich and meaningful, while their marriage often becomes a nightmare because of the routine, termination of admiration and adoration. If you want to win a Leo, you should ask him for protection, assistance, or praise him in bed like you have never experienced anything like it. They are able to listen carefully to what you tell them if they believe that they are actually chosen and important. They have much greater amount of energy and enthusiasm than other people, so they can often be a balm to the people who have experienced love traumas in the past, or some other life shipwrecks. If you had some interesting love experiences in the past, it would be best to record them in the diary and avoid an honest conversation about it. Sometimes it is necessary to withhold some things in love that will not help much in bed. If you want someone to take care of yourself, your family and your children, there is no better than Leo. They rarely let others down and they are ready to fight for love. If you are not willing to respect their quality or do not notice how loyal and special they are, then it is best not to enter into a relationship with them.

## Virgo - love and sexuality

When you read the astrological textbooks about Virgo, you gain the impression that they were born to repair and service, so we expect to find them with a wrench or some other tool in their pocket. This kind of discrimination is not entirely unjustified, but it should be emphasized that Virgo is not born just to work and serve. Although at some point in life they need solitude, renunciation and celibacy, we cannot say that they aren't capable of having romance, relationship or marriage. Some astrologers went so far to claim that Virgos are not attractive or beautiful, that they have no sex-appeal and how we cannot find anything specific or characteristic about them. The fact that Richard Gere, Greta Garbo and Sofia Loren were born in this sign makes us more cautious in categorizing people. Although they tend to withdraw and they seldom show self-initiative, we can notice that they can successfully resist and adapt to a variety of romantic crises and storms. This means that they can survive in marriages and in relationships despite adversities. Monasticism is linked to the sign of Virgo, so they must spend one part of life modestly, without some special love and erotic pleasures, which is about to change at one point in life. They prefer wise, prudent and serious partners and they like to serve, satisfy and be subordinated in bed and out of it. It rarely happens that they are dominant and offensive. Nevertheless, because of the excessive intellectual element, they strive to unusual relationships and we can often hear that they are inclined to the unusual sexual preferences. In marriage they are serious, responsible and loyal, good life partners and strict parents. They often give a lot for a tiny bit of love, and you do not have to try too hard around them. It rarely happens that they are truly happy, but there is a great dose of gratitude and loyalty. Sometimes sex life can be burdened with constant complaining, criticism and dealing with trivial matters. Virgos do not stand for imaginative lovers, but it can be overcome if in the horoscope there are strongly emphasized fifth, seventh and eighth field as well as love planets (Mars and Venus). If there is such a combination, be sure that you will be more than satisfied. Virgos often seek leaders, and show all kinds of obedience which can be considered an aphrodisiac in some way. It often happens that they are attracted to partners who are not special or handsome and end up in the unusual relationships or marriages. If you manage to free them from the discipline and modesty and gain their trust, they would be capable of fulfilling each of your desires which could further strengthen the relationship and sexual enjoyment in marriage. It is very important not to embarrass Virgo and not make her/him think that he/she is doing something wrong. People often do not realize that people write a lot about sex and love, but in practice few people can boast to live what we saw on the big screen, or read in the love manual.

## Libra - love and sexuality

This part of the Zodiac primarily talks about the relationships and the need to achieve them at any cost, so there is a constant need to find a partner and the inability to be single. For such a reason many relationship problems are created in time, and they are mostly not solved in the best way. Libra people often look good, regardless of whether they are male or female members of the sign, they have the need to be worshiped and seduced. They also enjoy the attention, flattery and gifts. On the other hand, some accuse them of being cold, forbearing and restrained, and that the icily, aristocratic heart beats under the beautiful facade.

Caution should be exercised in assessing a person's destiny, because it is not based only on the position of the Sun or the Ascendant (sub sign), but also the rest of the horoscope should be taken into account. If it happens that the Sun is in Libra, there is a high possibility that a person will be flirty, promiscuous, or will be inclined to the relationships which cannot be realized in practice. Somewhat smaller effect is in people who have the Ascendant (sub sign) in Libra, provided that the same are always looking for a leader in a partnership, marriage and in bed, therefore they suffer and eventually become embittered. If a person wants to have a beautiful, handsome partner with fine manners, who can serve as a decoration, a porcelain vase, or wants to impress friends, parents, and business partners, they should choose a person born in the sign of Libra, who meets all the conditions. The disadvantages of this sign are seen in the relationships which are not intimate, because Libra can be persuaded to anything. That is why their relationships and marriages suffer, because what Libra dare not say in company or at work, is sure to say at the family lunch or in bed. Their partners often say that they are nicer to strangers than to people with whom they have close relationships. On the other hand, Libra always knows what is good, knows how to enjoy, whether it's about choosing clothes, sit-ins, or traveling. They want great partners for themselves, but practice has shown that they end up with people who are totally different. Libra constantly needs love, attention, admiration, and the compliments are never too much. They have no need for excessive seclusion and celibacy like Virgo, and therefore end up in very strange and unusual relationships. Libra has a problem being single, so they often stumble upon 'Moonlighting' or people who seek refuge, safe haven or marriage. Libra is able to satisfy partner in bed, ready for games, experiments and seduction. We should never forget that Libra does not like to work much, nor has the need to be trapped in administration. If it happens that the partner can provide comfort, convenience and safety, they provide the maximum and are capable of being good parents, lovers and life partners.

# Scorpio - love and sexuality

Scorpio is truly the most intense of all the Zodiac signs, the toughest and the most passionate. This comes from the fact that Scorpio rules sexual organs and represents the zone of the Zodiac which seeks meaning of life through death, transformation and sexual union with another person. Scorpio corresponds to everything that bears the eighth house of the horoscope in itself, and it is in every way ready for the commitment in romantic relationships or marriage. These are the people who do not take anything for granted; they see or wish to see the deeper meaning in everything. They unconsciously require to "die for love" in every metaphorical sense, so they find partners who are totally eccentric, doctors, surgeons, artists, and people of strange and unimagined energy. Scorpio is quite tumultuous and restless in his own body, although to the observers it seems that they are calm and simple in a relationship. Due to dramatic conflicts that take place within them, they create relationships full of possessiveness, unbreakable or painful moments which often share the fate of the love affair between Isidore Duncan and the unfortunate poet Sergei Yesenin. Scorpio loves until death, loves theatrically like the musketeers in Dumas' novel, loves unreservedly, leaving nothing for tomorrow. Their loyalty can go to such an extent that they are capable of giving up any enjoyment as the sign of fidelity and loyalty. Due to the difficult character it happens that they experience severe disappointments, because people get tired from the intensity of such love. If you love a Scorpio, he will be grateful and loyal to the grave. If you hurt him, it can easily happen that he will turn into a resentful and restless river of hatred that will destroy everything in sight. In spite of everything being so, we often see Scorpio living in celibacy a certain period of time, particularly those with the Sun in Scorpio, while we don't have the same situation with people with Scorpio on the Ascendant (sub sign). Interestingly, Casanova and the Marquis de Sade were born with Scorpio in the Ascendant, which speaks of their over exaggerated sexual needs and desires. If they trust their partners these people show such need for sex and love experiments in which the other signs cannot compete them. Their quality is reflected in the essential understanding of the sexuality and their ability to make magic of the relationship. There is a strong need to prove, compete and take control in bed, so they are rarely seen as passive and less dominant. They are capable of surviving difficult times or adapting to less pleasant conditions in marriage or relationship. They are also willing to make love last long and rarely prefer adventures and little affairs which are the result of boredom. Scorpio has the desire to maintain a relationship and if they don't find themselves harmonious partners, their relationships become agony and struggle. If you enter into a love relationship with them, you should consider whether you have the strength to love until the end, and whether you are capable of giving over and surrendering completely.

## *Sagittarius - love and sexuality*

Astrologers are right when they say that Sagittarius is the luckiest sign, God's favorite. However, in this case to be happy doesn't mean to have a good relationship or harmonious marriage. Sagittarius enters emotional relationships in a much simpler, easier and more superficial way than the others and stays in them if their partners provide them enough freedom. When Sagittarius enjoys freedom, he is then able to provide the best and show all his qualities. Many complain that these people are too selfish, self-centered and often cold, which is not far from the truth. Since Sagittarius is a fire sign, people think that they fight for love fervently and equally devotedly in order to save it. Practice shows that this is not so. The advantage of this sign is that he/she seldom clearly shows jealousy and possessiveness, which contributes to the quality of the relationships, because they are spared of heavy and painful scenes that drain the energy and joy of life. They are thought to be good lovers, but they do not bother much, because they do not have the need to impress, amaze and leave the partners breathless. Sagittarius doesn't ask what the predecessor was like, because he doesn't burden himself with that, unlike Cancer and Scorpio who would give all to find out the juicy details from the past. The great strength of this sign is that they are well-intentioned, full of faith and optimism of a child, which is necessary for marriage or a serious relationship. Such optimism allows you to overcome the crises of life and love easily, which occur in cycles depending on the period of life. Sagittarius people suffer if they find a partner who is narrow-minded, primitive, harsh, tense and frustrated. He will not allow them be restricted or controlled, which can become a nightmare for the partners or spouses. They have enough self-esteem, nurture their bodies, recreate in sports, so they are often handsome, attractive and with the strained muscles. Sagittarius is rarely single, unlike Virgo, the devotee of the solitude and celibacy. In bed they usually settle their own needs and rarely ask what should be done to help partner get satisfied. Such an approach to sex and relationship can cause revolt, because one of the partners may feel exploited or neglected. Sagittarius is the ideal partner if you like to socialize, invite people to your home or have time for yourselves. They will rarely control and spy on others which gives enough space and freedom for additional activities. Although some claim that Sagittarius is traditional, we may often find them in scandals, affairs, double relationships in which they enter superficially, not wanting to jeopardize marriage. Sagittarius is hard to be attached to one person, which is somewhat good for them, but rarely feels good for the other side. If in the horoscope there is the additional emphasized water element (Cancer, Scorpio) or earth (Taurus), all those things could be mitigated and improved. It should be understood that astrology is much more serious matter of whether someone is Taurus or Cancer, so this analysis should be linked with the rest of the horoscope.

# *Capricorn - love and sexuality*

Some traditional astrologers have believed for centuries that Capricorn is the zone of the Zodiac in which there is a great interest in work and money, and a little less for love. They were also believed to be asexual and placed in the same basket along with Virgo. Such a conviction existed for the simple reason that Capricorn is quite cold by nature, slow and capable of suffering, but it does not mean that he is not passionate. On the other hand, we notice that the Zodiac signs are often generalized, so we often hear: "Ah, you are a Leo and you should seriously work on your ego," or "You Gemini people are so frivolous and superficial..." A similar fate befell Capricorns and we equally see the will and perseverance in them, the need to succeed and the desire for money. I've never heard that some astrologer connected this zone of the Zodiac with love pleasures and enjoyment. As a Capricorn represents a serious deterioration in the matter, it is easy to conclude that the money and status are closely related to sex, so we can find that these people have the exaggerated sexual needs, strength and endurance, but they are perhaps a little less romantic or less capable for the poetic inspiration. We have never seen a businessman who is romantic at the same time. In a few cases I have noticed that people with the emphasized Capricorn were striving for frequent sexual contacts which were not mandatory to the mutual enjoyment. We also find that women born in this sign can be very beautiful, especially when there is the planet Venus. Although it is a traditional sign which necessarily creates a home and family, these people can easily be caught in the infidelity and adultery. They hardly divorce, since they care much about what people think about their relationship or marriage. They are capable of staying with someone for decades, without love or intimacy in this connection. Capricorns will do anything to satisfy their sexual needs, and the partner does not have to be too good looking in order to come to the love act. On the other hand, they cannot cope with the infidelity and they can hardly overlook to find the partner in a stranger's bed. Capricorn is said to be an infertile sign, and yet we see them create large families and it is not uncommon for them to have more than two children. If there is also an emphasized Scorpio in the horoscope, they go to the extremes and try out things in bed which are quite strange and unusual. Capricorn has the need for the lasting marriage or relationship, which brings some kind of security and stability that, is necessary for a lot of people. They are rarely sentimental and especially dedicated in the relationship. On the other hand, they tend to be responsible when it comes to marital duties or obligations. Capricorn is not known for the foreplay, nor is particularly interested in the anatomy of the partner. Their quality is that they are not too sensitive or squeamish in bed, and having sex is a normal or natural thing for them, unlike Virgo, who is full of moral condemnation. It often happens that Capricorn enters into a relationship out of interest or the need to control the situation. We should not forget that these are true born leaders, who manage equally at work and in bed.

## Aquarius - love and sexuality

Aquarians enter into the love affairs and marriage with great zeal and enthusiasm, but soon realize that the field of the relationships is, in fact, a great enigma for them, and that by the end of their life they would remain the humble disciples. Aquarius is a sign which functions well in groups, collectives, when they have to fight for one's rights or conviction, however, in one-to-one relationship they become impetuous, weak and quite insecure. When you see an Aquarius (especially with the ascendant in Aquarius), you can feel free to ask: "You're divorced or you are planning to divorce?" There is no sign which tries harder to unite with somebody, but that doesn't work. The main problem is their gentle will that complements the powerful ego, and such a weakness is spotted very quickly in the emotional relationship. Aquarians are hardly made to persevere in something, so they show weakness and volatility, and when you ask them to bring you a glass of water, they automatically find that partner is trying to dominate and master them. Although Aquarius is a permanent and fixed sign ruled by Saturn, this zone of the Zodiac has no need for the union, but for the liberation. This "liberation" often results in divorce, insecure and unstable relationships, atypical sexual preferences, as well as the experiments that end ingloriously. Unlike Libra, Aquarius has no need for a leader or someone who would organize the life and activities. For that reason, they suffer terribly when they run into a person full of self-confidence, with a strong character, or people born in the signs of Aries, Leo or Capricorn. Their partners often condemn and accuse them of being more committed to the other's lives, than they are preoccupied with the relationship, marriage or any partnership. Also, there is a great misfortune in the fact that they cannot be closely united with one person. Aquarius often helps the salvation of the world, but never gets to help himself and his partner. On the other hand, Aquarians possess quite developed awareness when it comes to sexual needs, so they are able to satisfy many tastes. Taboo subjects hardly ever exist for them, so they are willing to test the limits of both their own and other people's sexuality. This is very important because we have already mentioned that sex is a prerequisite for the healthy and normal life. They are also in the mood for exploring, socializing, traveling and social life. These are the exceptional qualities of this sign, because sooner or later the passions subside, and it is necessary to enrich the life with new contents. Today many couples live modestly, quietly and inconspicuously with a can of sardines and chamomile tea, while Aquarians are able to enrich the life with the unusual encounters, significant contacts and going outs. Their main problem is how to become close with the person who is the most important in their life. They are the contrarians by nature, so they have the unconscious need to dispute the most stable claims. Why do they do that, no one has reliably found out yet. Although they are not capable of tolerating authorities, it is necessary for them to look for more reliable and stable partners in life.

# Pisces - love and sexuality

Pisces belong to the specific part of the Zodiac, which is little known of, yet the astrologers believe that they have studied it in detail, so when you open an astrological guide you can read how gentle they are, how caring, loving, ready to rescue the world from suffering and adversity. Immediately you expect that the majority of physicians were born in this sign and most of spiritual healers, which is proven to be incorrect. On the other hand, we read that Pisces are weepy, silent, and incapable of defending themselves against the others, who, ostensibly, drain their energy and steal their power. However, a large number of examinees agreed that they didn't experience marital happiness and harmony with people born in this sign, or that premarital relationships were filled with light things only, songs, music and enjoyment. Pisces belong to the zone of the Zodiac inclined to secrets, problems, emotional downs, so we can often see that the same are "sensitive, gentle and well-intentioned" people who do not act according to the astrological textbooks in love and relationships. Due to the specific delusion that they leave upon people, many are surprised when some embarrassment comes up, an affair gets out or it happens that they act in a strict, demanding and contentious way in marriage or relationship. Still more dust stirs up when they require things in bed and in sex which are rarely talked about, let alone performed in practice. The truth is that this is not the zone of the Zodiac which offers the maximum power, endurance and sexual potency, nor is it expected of them. However, we can often see that they tend to fantasize, tend to promiscuity and sexual perversions. Of course, if the rest of the horoscope includes some other element, it is almost certain that all of the above will be alleviated and weakened. Consciously or unconsciously Pisces incline to the people who will lead them, focus and steer them. In bed they are more obedient than they master or dominate. If there comes to the love or marital crisis, they suffer a lot and don't know how to govern the emotions. Mostly they are reproached for their instability, volatility and the secrets they carry in their heart. On the other hand, they are endlessly curious, enjoy gossiping and burden the partnership with unnecessary details. As this is a water sign, the truth is that they are able to develop deep and strong emotions, but we should not forget that Pisces correspond to the twelfth field of the Zodiac, which has a rather negative and vicious influence. A lot of psychological astrologers are persistently trying to incorporate the mediumistic abilities and the spiritual progress into this field, so all the dirt is thrown on Scorpios, who are treated as evil, full of wrath and anger, and Pisces should accordingly be merciful and infinitely grateful for the love and all they are provided in a relationship. The power of Pisces is that they have a different view on life and love, so it happens that they develop subtlety, intimacy or try to be kind, compassionate and romantic. They are not prone to self-initiative, but with a good partner they can develop deep and quality emotions. Pisces are not very demanding, so you do not have to spend money to save love, or the expensive gifts are not mandatory in order to satisfy them. As such, they can adapt to life's limitations and difficulties, which is extremely useful in a relationship. If they are tamed on time and directed towards higher values, Pisces become wonderful partners and good spouses someday.

*Note: these are just some of the characteristics of the signs of the Zodiac on the basis of which the natal horoscope cannot be interpreted, love and life expectancy assessed or anything alike. Astrology is much more than that. There is a way in which the natal horoscope is connected into a coherent whole. It is clear that not all Aries are brave nor all Cancers emotional and sensitive; therefore, we are talking about the Zodiac signs that possess certain qualities. It is important to understand that certain texts cannot be generalized nor the specific truths and statements established on their basis.*

# BUSINESS & MONEY

In addition to the fact that a man must feed and procreate by starting a family someday, an equally important part of life is his ability to gain money, organize and do something useful. All of us have different interests and aptitudes, as well as talents which differ from individual to individual. Each part of the Zodiac vibrates at a defined frequency and has certain strength, so we notice that some people are quick, choleric, and able to lead and the others lazy, sluggish, and sleepy and without initiative. By the deeper study of the Zodiacal signs we can understand better why one son is a capable mechanic, and a second in a poetic mood, gentle and lyrical.

## *Aries - business and money*

Aries is cardinal, positive, fiery sign which naturally carries the idea of leadership within. If you look more closely, you will realize that Aries are always bosses and rarely subordinates, porters, servants or office suppliers. They transmit the competitive spirit to work, and are stimulated if there are rivals, competitors, or seemingly better individuals near them. They work hard, spending a lot of energy. Aries don't know how to spare themselves and it happens that they fall from fatigue because everything they do, they do passionately and enthusiastically. This is also true for people with the Ascendant in Aries or stellium (more planets) in this sign. They perform their duties seriously and responsibly, but are not said to be team players; they create tension in the team regarding the position and the domination. If you want to hire an Aries, you can realistically expect him soon to leave the job because he found something better, more attractive and lucrative. However, Aries rarely make mistakes in the assessment so you may notice that by changing jobs and teams they really come to the head positions or you will be surprised to see them in a successful firm or company. They push themselves everywhere and literally speak about what they want without beating around the bush and without embellishing. This gives them a huge advantage over the insecure, withdrawn, introverted and shy people. While one Libra decides which term to use not to hurt the interlocutor, an Aries will take everything for himself without hesitation. They are grateful for the companies which need a firm hand because they are hard to be bribed or forced to change decision. Aries do all the work without much embellishment and often bang bumps to the disobedient or less capable workers. He doesn't need explanations how the salary is small, and the working conditions hard and unacceptable. If they believe that there is some Calimero injustice, they try to impose their will, and if they do not succeed they say goodbyes quickly, with no great sentimentality, looking for a better place under the Sun. It's a great thing when a man has the emphasized Aries in his horoscope because you can be sure that he will manage in every situation and you do not have to worry. And if there is an emphasized Earth element in the horoscope (especially Capricorn), their success and wealth is certain. Astrologers believe that this part of the Zodiac is corresponding to the energy sector, the defense industry, innovation, construction, technical sciences and management. If Aries accidentally finds himself in the art world, he would achieve a lot in television programs, pop-music, stage activities and show business. They also correspond to all forms of vigorous sports, the speed competition, individual sports, boxing, oriental martial arts and technical sports.

## *Taurus - business and money*

Unlike Aries, Taurus' primary energy is typically female, slow, sensuous and sensual, so it is astrologically classified into earthy, fixed (i.e. slow or difficult to change), the female character. Taurus really has no need to compete, doesn't burn out at work, nor is consumed to the last atom of strength. It is a very cunning, material sign, so we notice that they are neither the best workers nor the pioneers in any job, but in most cases in life they build financial stability and security. By doing some research I noticed that Taurus lived as tenants in the fewest number of cases and it usually happened that in later years of life they were quite wealthy. This also applies to the people with Taurus in the Ascendant, or most of the planets in the same sign. Since this is a sluggish, inert and melancholic part of the Zodiac, Taurus has developed the motto "do not work, but earn", and with a little effort recognizes how the money is gained, piled up and multiplied. Where the other people see a huge gaining, Taurus only sees a small percentage of the profits. They are practical, fundamental and calm; they do not rush into all undertakings and are not pushed by the business adventurism from situation to situation. In this way they save energy and operate where the situation is clear and concrete. This gives them time to organize themselves, since they are patient and hard to enter into something that is not absolutely clear. In this way they are often spared the scams, bankruptcy and businesses that resemble the betting style - wait for it to come from ace to deuce. Taurus people do not need to be the best; they are not particularly inspired to stand at the helm of businesses, enterprises, nor are pushing to become spokesmen and managers. This part of the Zodiac is satisfied with the financial stability, peace and tranquility. If the properties are numbered, the business is good, the taverns full of guests, then these people feel that the mission is accomplished and that life does not need to be particularly complicated by the intricate actions and situations. Everything that is related to agriculture, botany, science, trade-financial area, banking (Taurus people are often cash-collectors or bankers), trade, horticulture, agriculture, design, art, building, cooking, pastry cooks industry, cosmetics, accessories, painting, sculpture, theater, singing (planets in Taurus give a very strong voice, except for the planet Mars) and architecture, can be found in the sign of Taurus. It is therefore necessary to develop these fields, cherish them and finally live happily from your own work. People have the need to do what they have seen from the others or read somewhere, enroll schools because they have best friends from the elementary there, or catch the microphone because there are numerous auditions. Astrology only helps people discover their affinities, because rare indeed are those who do what they love, who know their job, and finally make a good living from it.

## *Gemini - business and money*

I once talked about how astrology became quite fun lately, so we can often hear: "Oh, he's a Gemini, fickle and hypocritical" or "Yes, he is a Leo, so he has now imagined being Napoleon." Although there are certain similarities with what people perceive, you can easily run into a Gemini who is moody, withdrawn and quiet, as well as a Leo who is insecure and without self-confidence. This is because astrology is much more than about the position of the Sun sign or a mere belief that Virgos are diligent and Taurus lazy. Gemini belongs to the intellectual part of the Zodiac along with some other signs, it is a variable sign (i.e. shifty and flexible), and male (has the need to be publicly and directly expressed) and airy (thoughtful, intellectual, the flux of ideas and observations...). We can often read in the astrological texts that Gemini should write books, and yet we see that Dostoyevsky, Tolstoy, Balzac, Zola and many other giants of the world literature have nothing to do with this sign. Gemini people are excellent in jobs which require skill, dynamism and flexibility. They easily solve complex, intricate and complicated situations with the innocent, childlike joy and enthusiasm, which, unfortunately, does not last long. They are good at jobs that require mediation, lightness and airiness. All that is intriguing, new, exciting and does not require the excessive muscular work, absolutely corresponds to this sign. Gemini people are not the darlings of the pickaxe and shovel, and they do not enjoy the company of people who think slowly and have difficulties in expressing themselves. They learn easily and they're brilliant during the first weeks at work, but very soon they lose will and freshness and seek satisfaction in another job. They are often unreliable workers, because a seat doesn't hold them long. They are asking questions frequently, and every answer obtained is followed by the new question. Since Gemini people are the victims trapped in their own bodies, they strive to the jobs which are not stereotyped, they do not enjoy in everyday stamping, folding papers, working on the line that carries the screws, nor rejoice to the responsible jobs that require patience, discipline and precision. Of course, if the rest of the horoscope is quite powerful, all those things are greatly reduced and weakened. If they find themselves in the world of medicine, they should be interested in psychotherapy and any other type of therapy. If they are particularly intrigued by art, it would be desirable to have interest in choreography, graphics, painting and satirical literature. In sports, they might find satisfaction in volleyball, basketball and athletics. If we study better this part of the Zodiac, we find that Gemini people are successfully operating in the brokerage business, publishing activity, book trade, journalism, business news, translation services, transport, all types of communication, small business, commercial activities and any other that require a sharp and fresh intellect, new startup ideas, diversity and resourcefulness. Gemini is able to connect in business the extremely strict, rigid and reserved people with the innovators, pioneers and all those that are adorned by the original ideas and futuristic spirit.

## Cancer - business and money

Part of the Zodiac that involves the sign of Cancer is very vulnerable and sensitive, and many modern astrologers believe that the same astrological zone accounts for the largest part of human kindness and the ability to empathize with others. In spite of that, Cancer, along with Scorpio, are dead-heating over who forgives harder and who is harder to recover from the injustices and injuries inflicted upon them. The reason for this kind of emotional suffering lies in the truth that water signs experience everything in a subjective way, so every problem at home, at work or anywhere on the globe is intimately tied to them. Therefore, Cancers feel much better in the private sector and the personal property, so often we see that they are self-organized in operating their own business. Once in the team, they become over attached to the colleagues, staff or the superiors, so they get hurt in the stressful situations because someone disappointed them or was rude to them. They are incapable of getting rid of the impressions, images and memories from the past. Cancers get more and more closed and can hardly swim in the stressful society where changes are frequent and the great dynamism and tension are expected. They can be very thankful if you pay your attention to them or the work is imbued with emotions which are not strictly related to the job. The same goes for the people who are born with many planets in Cancer or have Cancer in the ascendant. Due to the excessive sense of privacy with society, roots and the exaggerated patriotism, we often come across Cancers in the state and military apparatus, as well as the police. If the job is stressful and the commitments numerous, Cancer is taking the ailments and troubles from work straight home, and in the worse variant their health suffers. This is certainly the most fragile part of the Zodiac, so the vicious diseases and tumors are called just after this sign (Cancer). Cancers know how to be responsible and loyal, dedicated and enterprising, as long as they are not threatened or threatened by some sort of injury. After that they shut themselves, treat themselves on their own and heal their wounds, which can last very long. This can be a problem, because a job suffers and the relationships are disturbed. Cancers are good in the security and property jobs, small and large trade, working with children and people, activities related to food and drink (catering, services), housework (various skills, tools, plumbing, working with all elements of kitchen...), as well as some forms of public activities. If a Cancer is found in medicine, it would be desirable to have an interest in psychotherapy (because he feels people and their problems and develops closeness and empathy), pulmology (Cancer next to Gemini rules the lungs), pediatrics (because he loves children) and parapsychology (because this is the occult part of the Zodiac). If they found themselves in the art world, it would be desirable to be interested in music, theatre and painting. If a

Cancer is interested in education and science, it would be good to deal with geography, history, archeology, botany, economics and military sciences.

## Leo - business and money

Leo is one of the happiest and brightest, the glaring part of the Zodiac that harmoniously and coherently links the fire elements (Aries and Sagittarius), and therefore gets the most out of life. Leos are definitely not the best, nor superior to the other people, but the fate somehow seems to find them in the best places. This counts for those who have the emphasized Leo (Napoleon, Caesar, Madonna, Sean Penn, Alexander Dumas, Robert Redford...), Ascendant in Leo (Meryl Streep...) or the ruler of the horoscope in Leo (Michael Jackson, Hemingway, Charlie Sheen, Julia Roberts, Roger Federer, Paulo Coelho...). This setup of things impels even a laic to conclude that these people have achieved something special, above expectations and have left an indelible impression about their life on Earth. How a Leo is a field of creativity and creative energy, he has absolutely no business being in clerical jobs, bureaucracy and paperwork. His nature tends to express itself publicly, enthusiastically, strongly and directly. Leo is the fixed, male, fiery sign that wants to share with the rest everything that follows him in life (success, joy, sadness...). Since he puts everything in his life in public, he also acquires powerful enemies. Such hostility can often be noticed when he enters the adult world and tries to make progress there. At work he tends to be authentic and striking, with the strong dramaturgical elements, and people are sometimes bothered by his fierce energy, pompousness, pride and theatricality. In spite of it, a Leo is able to remain in one workplace long and to storm the challenges, crises and difficult days. Truly, he has no pleasures in a subordinate position, nor is he looking forward to be the second. We often see that he moves forward, no matter what kind of work it is about. It rarely happens that a Leo fails, that he's neglected or lives in the shadow of events.

If they respect the authorities and co-workers they can become appreciated and very popular. They are also ready to assist in work, if their assistance is treated as necessary and important. They want to be respected, so they are generous as bosses, supervisors and organizers. If a Leo wants to be the best (whatever that means in the material world) he accomplishes it without much effort or embellishment. At work he may be responsible or punctual if he achieves the harmonious relationship with the team. They are authentic in politics (Fidel Castro, Benito Mussolini...), management and education. If a Leo finds himself in the art world, it is necessary to be interested in literature (achieves incredible success with an average writing), show-business, stage performance, film, directing and theatre. In the world of medicine a Leo should be interested in massage, pediatrics, cardiology, cardiac surgery and rehabilitation. They can also succeed in the organization of courses and schools, various trainings, presentations, working with gold and gems, auctions, stock exchange and pyramidal operations, hairdressers' and fashion salons. A Leo must never forget that all he got by birth represents the divine creation. Through this sign of the Zodiac we see how magnificent the will of the Creator was.

## *Virgo - business and money*

Virgos pass through the whole life modestly, quietly and inconspicuously, with the conspicuous desire to serve, satisfy and execute commands and tasks. It needs much effort to invest in order that a Virgo understands that she is equal and even with other people. The same applies for those who have the accentuated Virgo in personal horoscopes (more planets) or the Ascendant in Virgo. If you wish to find a good, meek, conscientious and disciplined worker, who doesn't ask for much, who is able to tolerate objections and criticism, who comes right on time, never forgets his duties and responsibilities, then be sure to hire a Virgo. If you are ambitious and fear that you could be overcome by your worker, that he could dazzle you and take a piece of glory from you, then again you should employ a Virgo. However, you should choose Virgos, because they work much and find happiness only in work. You will rarely meet a Virgo hedonist, light-handed, eager to enjoy rest and relax. This zone of the Zodiac is particularly related to the duties, sacrifices, analysis and a kind of loneliness and isolation, which is less noticeable when these people are busy and do not have much time to remain alone with their thoughts. Virgo is grateful in this greedy world, where everyone has an exaggerated ego, starting from a modest dairy man who delivers orders in the morning to the higher structures (managers, politicians, businessmen...), because he will not ask for much, does not bother to clear the foreground, rarely asking for a raise, does not grumble and does not complain, and does not take someone else's credits for himself. Virgo is also grateful for the places where you have to be active, alert and vigilant, so as not to lead to some big mistake and failure. You do not need to repeat to a Virgo at the end of the day that the machines should be switched off, that the lights should be checked and the key removed from the car in the parking lot. These people are capable of carrying out both even the most complicated and the smallest, pedant actions, that the others cannot feel. Due to the strong desire to help and serve, we often find them in the world of medicine, pharmacy, therapy, teaching activities and all other works which require modesty, composure and soberness. Virgos excel incredibly in the exact sciences (mathematics and physics), in journalism (first degrees of Virgo), pedagogy and psychology, languages (especially in the twentieth degree of Virgo), medicine, pharmacology, veterinary medicine and accountancy, bureaucratic jobs, printing and book publishing activities, librarian jobs, repairing things, furniture and small items, as well as housework. In medicine, they are prominent in hygiene, homeopathy, therapy, dietetics and pharmacology. If you want Virgos to work even better, it is necessary to reward them, to praise them and to emphasize their virtues which they have revealed quietly. We should never forget that the small and humble people are often the most responsible for a project, invention or work, as they create patiently in the shadow and it often happens that their work is never noticed nor praised. One king would have never been so magnificent in his luxurious quarters, if it weren't for many servants who work for him day and night. We should think about it sometimes.

## Libra - business and money

Unlike Virgo, people born in the sign of Libra are unwilling or incapable of doing any job. Some will reproach them for that and accuse them of being too sophisticated, but it will not change their philosophy of life much. We often hear that Libra, supposedly, always "weighs" something, which has little to do with their basic nature. The part of the Zodiac which Libra covers (especially the first fifteen degrees) is quite refined, and the members of this sign just do not like to get their hands dirty, nor want to be exposed to the excessive exertion. We can often read that Libra is too emotional, which is really far from the truth, still they cannot be denied good manners, courtesy and amiability. Since these people like admiration, attention and dedication from others, we often find them in public life where they feel the best. If Libra is not at the front positions, or depends on the will and mercy of bosses and superiors, they often suffer because they lack the courage to ask for a raise, to say what they really think and feel, so they enter into the unpleasant situations. Due to their indecision, lack of confidence and hesitancy, often the closest members suffer (the partner and family) because everything that Libra doesn't dare to tell the boss, dares to tell the family members. It is easy to make Libra stay a few hours longer at work, because he/she is not able to defend himself/herself, so she piles up the rage and anger within, because of the desire to please the others. Libra people are often favored because they want to know all, they are well-informed, they know where everything can be bought and at what price, so they create numerous business friendships that foster the spurious feelings.

A Libra likes to be present at the trendy places and is happy to cooperate with people who are respected and appreciated. If a Libra is not fulfilled in business or less successful, she often participates in business intrigues, but rarely draws the short end. Libra people are capable of showing kindness even to the competitors, which is a huge advantage in the world of business, unlike Cancers and Scorpios which you can face-read for every violation or disagreement. They are good in consulting, assessment and expertise, design, architecture and everything associated with the art. People born in the sign of Libra are often the best hairdressers, makeup-artists, clothing designers and photographers. At an early age they are recognized for their talent for decoration, sculpture, painting and show-biz scene. They enjoy connecting people, so they opt for the legal affairs, social services and conventional social activities. Libra is the best ambassador for the arts and culture because she has a refined taste for beautiful and is rarely fooled when it comes to choosing a quality literary reading, film or a painting. When it comes to the sports, we find them in figure skating and gymnastics, dance and athletics. Since life of every man is often filled with bitter and unpleasant moments (loss, illness, disappointment...) the part of the Zodiac that Libra covers, shows to the people that in addition to work and service there is also time for break (film, music, theatre...), beauty (manicure, hair salons and beauticians...), socializing and connecting people. This world is much nicer and more pleasant when there are people who create and make the rest feel better, at least for a while.

## Scorpio - business and money

Scorpios do not enjoy the best reputation among the astrologers, and laymen also often use term "jealous Scorpio", so when this sign is mentioned, the others step back thinking that what hides behind is a cunning, sly and not very pleasant person. Such an attitude towards Scorpio is not completely undeserved, and there are good reasons for that. Such an image brings a problem at the workplace, to the bigger or lesser team, because the world is divided into good and bad people, positive and negative, those who inspire us and those who steal our energy and exhaust us. Scorpios, in the opinion of many, fall into the latter group. In spite of everything, they are held for the successful, powerful and magnetic people, with the steadfast will and the fixed targets which they follow to the exhaustion. Such people never give up and do not easily change course in life. Everything they imagine they achieve through a long, stubborn and fierce battle. Nothing ever falls from the sky for a Scorpio, and when they get hold of the desired goal, they cleverly decide on tactics and defend their position. They cannot function without the enemy, and if the enemy doesn't really exist, a Scorpio will create them for itself. Moreover, they progress better and faster when they are convinced that someone is trying to thwart their plans. Scorpio is a fanatical follower of his goal, but on the road to success he goes through with a lot of injuries, pain, unresolved interpersonal relationships... Honestly, it is not good to have them as enemies, because they can be obsessed with some sick idea and they never forget their opponent. Scorpio has the power to attract and suck energy, and he is poorly adapted to the team because he thinks everyone is against him or that there is collusion. They do not believe the others and like to take control of everything. Scorpios are particularly quiet people and they come to the finish line by working and planning it all well. The arrival of a Scorpio in a company (especially people with the Ascendant in Scorpio) is a sign of terrible changes in the team (many are retiring, some are fired, and the company is moving to another location, the owner of the company starts a new project...). What many do not know is that Scorpios do not come in peace, nor intend to serve the others; they come to win and be the first. The strength of this sign is the endless patience and the fierce energy that lies behind their kindness (female sign), fine manners and the strength of the overflowing river. Although we are talking about the sensitive water sign, we could say that it is about the boiling hot water capable of dissolving and flooding all on its way. If you enter into business with them, you can count on loyalty, but you should always choose words wisely and think out the business move, so that the Scorpio would not imagine that it was conspiracy. If that happens, your real troubles are only beginning. On the other side they are durable, responsible, straining to the maximum and do not give in when it is difficult. They are also able to take responsibility and set themselves as protectors when needed. They can change the business environment, but are also able to stay long in one place, which is not particularly convenient. Scorpio always goes where it's time to switch something off and metaphorically die, and to build a new house, company or city in the same place. They never come in the team by chance, and when they show up you should know that it is time for the purge, reorganization and the new beginning. Scorpios can be found in criminology, chemical industry, security and control, banking (insurance, pawns...), military industry, funeral services... If they enter into the world of medicine they are concerned with pathology, surgery, urology, gynecology, psychiatry and parapsychology. In literature they leave a deep mark due to the Faustian outlook on life (Dostoevsky, Edgar Allan Poe, and Turgenev, in art (Paganini, Strauss, Picasso...) and in the world of film (Grace Kelly, Rock Hudson, Charles Bronson, Katherine Hepburn and many others). They do everything with great intensity, passionately and fanatically. The others remember them as the uncompromising and completely devoted to the goal.

## Sagittarius - business and money

Sagittarius is the only sign of the Zodiac, which is fully capable of rejoicing with the others when their life is going fine. If you say to a Sagittarius that you've opened a company or started a new business, you will automatically get a reply that it is great news and he will selflessly give you the useful advice in this regard. However, if you say the same thing to a Scorpio, her first reaction would be the internal injury, and then the pondering how this newly created company could be threatening for her own positions. Because of kindness and sincerity, a Sagittarius is favored and often loved by people because he believes that there is sufficient space under the sky for him also. Although it is a fiery, male, variable sign, a Sagittarius is often cold, and honestly not interested in the other people's lives and destinies. This is a great advantage, because he is not burdened, he does not waste resources and does not peek at someone else's yard. His weakness is the excessive faith and the unreasonable enthusiasm that leads him to business failures, adventurism and financial losses. He also quickly gives up projects because he runs out of patience and perseverance. A Sagittarius changes decisions fast, sees life widely, brightly and futuristically, confident that he can overcome any obstacle or business problem. Where the feverish Virgo sees small profits and bankruptcy, a Sagittarius always sees success, wealth and profit. Such things cost him a fortune, and he often starts from the scratch, again caught by the good faith and convinced that he's sailing under the full sails on a big wave. I guess God too has compassion when he sees with what fervor Sagittarius people go through life. Good life circumstances that accompany these people bring them to be average and mediocre workers. It always comes from the gifts that have fallen from heaven, on which the suffering Scorpio sincerely envies him. Sometimes it is enough for a Sagittarius to make contact, dial several phone numbers and after that you can see him in a successful company or doing a good job. Being the darling of the skies, many times he does not use his maximum, but flirts with the conditions depending on the needs. This does not mean that they cannot be good workers. However, the good life circumstances make people's spirit die, they put people to sleep and make them lazy. It is always easier to enjoy than to work hard, to storm the windmills and fight to survive. For this reason, Sagittarius shows no signs of jealousy and has no need for competing and taking high positions. Although many books on astrology speak of the spiritual side of this sign and the accented religiosity, more often we can see a Sagittarius hedonist than a Sagittarius monk in skimpy costumes rotating his rosary and praying for good crops. Sagittarius can be found in higher education, politics, ministry departments, publishing activities, international companies, big business, tourism, sports, transport, wholesale, marine, shipbuilding, religion and justice. Living abroad is a Sagittarius' natural thing, they tend to have foreign contacts or have the opportunity to work in foreign companies. Since many things in life they get easily done, it is necessary to put more effort, exercise persistence and avoid last-minute operations. Sagittarius was not born to suffer, have difficulties and walk on thorns. Therefore, they should not be blamed, because everything that one gets in life are the sincere gifts and wish of the Creator.

## Capricorn - business and money

Capricorn belongs to the part of the Zodiac which is strictly related to the substance and creation. These people can be practical and capable of making two pounds from one. During the lifetime they try to gain as much as possible but patiently and carefully. They are skilled in management, organization and planning. It is believed that they succeed in mid-life and that in the old age they sometimes achieve a considerable success at a time when many have disposed of their spears, ready for fishing, napping and taking care of grandchildren. Capricorn often does things systematically, saving energy, deciding on tactics, but never stands out too much. They carefully observe the ways to achieve success and build their careers with patience and calm. The other signs of the Zodiac often cannot keep up or get lost in the sea of obstacles and problems. Capricorn tries not to create many enemies, he's not suffocating convincing others that they are guilty, but tries to take enough for himself, provide for himself or acquire any sort of security. These people are particularly agile in business, practical and clever. I often saw Capricorns who held several trades in their golden hands. Some will find them fault that they are cold and strictly dedicated to the goal, but it can be observed only by those who know Capricorns. Although astrological textbooks talk about the slow, cool and sluggish sign, hard life and depression, we often notice that Capricorns push everywhere, make new acquaintances, calculate and vigilantly come to the desired positions. During the lifetime they try to create a family, build a house and earn money. Because of this attitude they often neglect other aspects of life, so they do not develop in all directions. No matter how it seems inferior compared to the dominant signs of the Zodiac, a Capricorn can surprise with a good and expensive car, a big house or a sizable bank account. They are ready to work hard jobs, but always see a chance for something better or try to change something. Capricorn is capable of changing course all of a sudden, of starting something new; he suddenly leaves the company or makes a major life change. This happens because he belongs to the cardinal signs along with Aries, Cancer and Libra, who initiate the action and have a driving energy that is activated depending on the business moment. They acquire the business wisdom and spend their time wisely, do not waste power and know how to organize people. It all basically covers the desire for success and achievement in a deft and patient manner. So, it is about the hard workers who stand firmly on the ground. Due to the dark and melancholic temperament they can be narrow-minded and stingy, believing that the only remedy and salvation is in cash, in the leading position or in friends who have achieved a lot. Sooner or later, a Capricorn always comes to the desired position. If in the horoscope there is a component of Scorpio, they can live long. When they gain enough money they do not squander, live modestly sharing advice to the others, even if a Capricorn gets rich during the lifetime, he will never reveal that he is happy, untroubled and satisfied. We can find them in the state insurance and security, ministry, civil service, the managing apparatus, politics, various crafts, building, architecture, heavy physical work, selling old and used things, agriculture and many other occupations.

# Aquarius - business and money

Here it is about the talented and original people. When the astrologers speak of Aquarius they often mention the reformatory spirit, desire for freedom and independence, but rarely about how difficult it is for the Aquarians to fit into the team, exactly because of the specific, independent and restless nature. They do not necessarily have to be geniuses, as some authorities in astrology claim; what they have is a swift and incisive intelligence, as well as the ability to see things much more clearly than the others. During their lifetime they develop a special view of the world, strengthen the spirit, unable to come to terms with many things. For this reason they are not the favorites of bosses, neither the good consorts with people who have achieved a lot in a suspicious and rather vague manner. All they do is colored by the strong need for independence, which is not preferred in the team work, company or a larger collective. Aquarius (especially those with Ascendant in Aquarius) in some moments can particularly shine progress far from the others and achieve a great deal. Unfortunately, they don't have the strong strategy and will, nor are ready to go to the end at any cost. It often seems that they go from one extreme to another, so in one moment their work is brilliant, and in another they show boredom and indifference. This is particularly reflected in creative people and artists. Although they do not show the excessive desire for the accomplishment, an Aquarius is difficult to tame and they generally provide a strong resistance when the coercion, domination or the strict rules are imposed upon them. They often help the others, strive to fulfill the promises given and show a remarkable level of understanding of other people's weaknesses. Although it is widely said that the Aquarians are fighting for the human rights, it would be best to let them create their own future. Aquarians are able to create new world, new trends, they are the originators of many movements, able to link the disparate things and understand the events that will occur many years later. Their lives are filled with constant changes, breaks and fights for the better future. They are convinced that the world will be a much better place one day, happier, and the people selfless, loving, tolerant and understanding. Aquarians often struggle for the Utopian issues, so they lose a lot of energy storming the windmills, explaining to the people that there is enough food and money for all; explaining that it is not good to eat and kill animals, and many other things that distract them from the professional growth and advancement. Aquarians are by default not greedy or rapacious. Although Saturn rules the signs of Capricorn and Aquarius, there is a big difference in the basic nature of these two signs. Aquarius rarely falls low because of the work, money, social position and status. If it happens that in the lifetime they do not achieve the things they dreamed of, or their lucky star never shines, they can retreat, isolate, seclude and become strange. Aquarians have the strongest sense of people and can best understand what the harmony, understanding, tolerance and kindness mean to the world. What should be specifically emphasized is their incredible sense for music, literature and art, so we find that the following people were born in the sign of Aquarius: Mozart, Artur Rubinstein, Lord Byron, Stendal, Jules Verne, James Joyce, Charles Dickens, James Dean, Paul Newman, Bob Marley, Bertold Brecht, Edison, Adler, Darwin, Schubert, Edgar Mone, and many others. An Aquarius is found in the technical sciences, cybernetics, nuclear physics, inventing, energy, electronics, aviation, internet technology. If they are interested in medicine, it would be good to try themselves in neurology, homeopathy and psychotherapy.

## *Pisces - business and money*

Pisces belong to the water signs (along with Cancer and Scorpio), and their common feature is that they are in touch with their feelings which others often do not even notice. Like the other water signs, Pisces experience everything with the powerful impressions, and their actions are colored by deep emotions. In mythology Pisces is associated with Derceto who threw herself into the sea to avoid the suffering of the everyday life and plunged into the world of fantasy, unreal and dreamy. Due to that, the sea god Poseidon punished her and turned her into a mermaid - half fish and half woman. The mythological story of the sign of Pisces is associated with the escape from reality, utopian ideas, and the world of fantasy, imagination and art. One would think that Pisces do not cope well in the material world, which may not be entirely true. Many times I have mentioned that for the assessment of fate, the rest of the Zodiac should be taken into account and it is not enough to know whether a person is born in the sign of Aquarius or Pisces. Because of the dual nature (one side facing the material pleasures and the other side completely imaginary and hypersensitive), Pisces are going through the grueling life lessons trying to adapt as better. They are capable of making sacrifices, shouldering the burden, working more, or taking responsibility for the others, listening carefully and empathizing with people. Their kindness or naivety is widely used by the individuals who leave early from work, campaign workers, who transfer the part of the responsibilities to the others. Astrology has divided people into the "higher" and the "lower" types where the higher types show maximum quality, they're honest, responsible and brave, and the lower slander, do not fulfill their obligations and demonstrate the weakness of the respective sign. So with the people born in the sign of Pisces, we can get to know the higher types, who are missionaries, leaders, willing to help the others, encourage them and strengthen, create masterpieces and the lower types who shirk, being drawn into the intrigues and showing a sick curiosity. The advantage of people born in the sign of Pisces over the other water signs (Cancer and Scorpio) is that they cannot hide their true emotions (fear, anger, suspicion, possessiveness, insecurity...), which gives them a big advantage at work. The responsible for this kind of concealment is the planet Neptune, which is the co-ruler of this sign and symbolizes secrets and imaginary world. In this way Pisces are able to protect themselves and often spare themselves from the further suffering and the inconvenience. This part of the Zodiac rules everything that has to do with the organic chemistry, fluids, oil, beauty salons, pharmacies, beautiful things, photography, work related to the treatment (hospitals and sanatoriums), video and audio industry, musical instruments, theatre, music, poetry, psychology, art theory, aesthetics and all the other creative activities. The important representatives of the twelfth sign of the Zodiac are Chopin, Michelangelo, Handel, Victor Hugo, Albert Einstein, Elizabeth Taylor and many others.

> *Note: these are just some of the characteristics of the signs of the Zodiac on the basis of which the natal horoscope cannot be interpreted, love and life expectancy assessed or anything alike. Astrology is much more than that. There is a way in which the natal horoscope is connected into a coherent whole. It is clear that not all Aries are brave nor all Cancers emotional and sensitive; therefore, we are talking about the Zodiac signs that possess certain qualities. It is important to understand that certain texts cannot be generalized nor the specific truths and statements established on their basis.*

# CHILDREN - ZODIAC SIGNS

## *Aries child (sign & ascendant)*

You should not be overly worried for these children. They master the lessons of life very early, mingle and meet with the other children and quickly attempt to impose their leadership, in a way that they easily overpower the others, regardless of the disciplines. An Aries child is not much aware of the other children, so they naturally have no desire or need to be subordinated. They are full of energy, vitality and lust for life. If their competitive spirit is not restrained, it may even happen that the society rejects them or shies away from them. From an early age they should be taught to save and preserve energy, because later in life they can get rather exhausted and worn out. This particularly reflects on their health and shape as the time passes. Ever since the early childhood they should be taught to take plenty of fluids so that later they wouldn't suffer inflammations, headaches and sinuses. An Aries child often does not know for equity and equality and has the need to share lessons or impose leadership. This approach creates a lot of trouble later. Children born in the sign of Aries exhibit different abilities very early; they are rarely rigid, they perform directly and openly, being friendly and impartial. They often say what they think which in practice proved to be a problem, because many do not want that someone pushes the truth under their noses. In the early youth and childhood, compassion, attention, patience, as well as the access to the authorities should be developed. Aries children do not like authorities and exhibit the innate resistance, so that later, if they are not bosses at work, they are mainly self-employed or unemployed because they cannot fit into the team. Teamwork is the Achilles' heel for the child born in this sign since they need to bang bumps and provide guidelines. They neither should be closed in the room, nor their spite awaken. If a parent tries to crush the spirit of such a child violently, it later gives birth to anger, hostility, cruelty and the unpleasant character. They are rarely born as possessive and jealous because they believe that they are faster, more capable and more agile than the other children. They early express the love for technical sciences. The more love they receive in the early childhood, more easily will they give love, because they know to be rough in the appearance, so later they suffer in marriage or a relationship. Dynamism and action are inherent in these children, they lead in the development and later it is easier and simpler to them to pave their way through life. When their development is carefully approached, they become precious leaders and the authorities simple and easy to follow. They are always capable of accepting both the responsibility and the guilt. They rarely suppress their feelings within themselves.

## *Taurus child (sign & ascendant)*

A child born in the sign of Taurus is very different than a child born in the sign of Aries. By nature it is somewhat slower, more sluggish and inert. This does not mean that they do not have energy, only they do not express their nature directly and explosively, but they need to hold wishes, needs or emotions. It is difficult to get them angry, so they easily accept other children into their company and it is not important to them to be the best, the first, special or rewarded. For this reason, they often in childhood preserve the nerves and the patience for the old age, and we come to the phlegmatic and really benign persons. It would be good for them to be early involved in sports, or that the need for routine is instilled in their childhood in some way, since they prefer lounging and enjoying. Many times these are really beautiful, talented and creative children who need more time because, simply, they do not have such a strong initiative.

It is difficult for them to opt for the action, but they can be quite persistent if they pounce on their goal. They must learn from the early age that flexibility, variability and adaptability often contribute that the human copes well in different situations. Since they are not particularly prone to sudden changes and abrupt decisions, it happens many times that other children take "a better or bigger cake" or they impose themselves better in school and society. Since they are strongly related to desires, inner needs and substance, they should be taught to earn their money early, or to turn the ideas into practice. They should also be showed that there is a dual personality in a man - one that tends to God and the other that tends to gaining wealth. Spiritual principles and the emphasized religiosity are the true enigma for such children, so one day they become the great entrepreneurs and builders, and on the other hand they do not believe that beyond this life there might be something more. Such simplicity and convenience eventually become a problem, especially if they grow up in an environment where the parents are particularly religious or spiritual. They need to be weaned from the heavy food, candies, hedonism and enjoyment. They start to feel their body early, so they enter into serious and deep relationships even in puberty.

## *Gemini child (sign & ascendant)*

These children are lively, cheerful, happy, very agile and busy. It is easy to deal with them and it is easy to "tame" them because they have great intelligence, curiosity and need to learn through the acquisition of data which they quickly "analyze" and reject at the same speed. They, unfortunately, lack focus and stability, so in addition to the sharp intelligence and ease of learning they do not have routine, which reflects negatively later in life. Such children need to be directed or limited from the early age, because they are capable of learning anything and are often carried away. We notice that they easily achieve the desired results, and do not make a special effort nor they burn over the book. Later, we see that they finish serious schools with just a little notebook in their hands. The excessive curiosity and desire for acquiring informational experiences makes them superficial in everyday life. For this reason, in mature years they move from job to job, changing habits, trying to find something worthy of long attention. Wherever the play, entertainment, current events are - they are also there. They should be offered the opportunity to work and adopt more complex life lessons to find the life's calling more easily. They are of gentle health and less resistant. Their lungs are somewhat weaker in childhood and the plantain tea or syrup is ideal in order to get them more resistant in the mature age. They rarely have enemies, because during childhood they accept anybody without dividing people into good and bad. Everything is fun to them, so they get hurt often during growing up, since they realize late that life is not a game. They have an innate gift for writing, speaking, communication, adapt easily to others and they are not vengeful. They are perfunctory in many jobs, yet in the same time unique and brilliant. Their problem is that their attention is scattered, and they find it difficult to pursue a goal. Something that concerns them at the moment becomes a memory and the oblivion the next moment. It would be ideal if they could learn foreign languages from the early age, because they are capable of memorizing incredible things. It should be noticed from their early childhood in which area they lead, and they should not be allowed to change their routes just because they are bored or the same thing no longer entertains them. The universe has rewarded these children because they know how to rejoice small things sincerely and selflessly and innocently enjoy everything offered. After all, all our existence comes down to a few moments that mean life.

## Cancer child (sign & ascendant)

These children are warm, gentle, compassionate, possessively attached to the loved ones and full of deep and incomprehensible emotions. Children born in the sign of Cancer do not need to be specially taught how to love or feel the others. They develop empathy for other people easily, but they are also excessively binding and such an attachment over time results in possessiveness, jealousy and strange feelings. This is particularly noticeable in families where the parents are divorced or estranged. It is difficult for them later to accept others in the family environment because of vulnerability and the fear of being hurt. From their early age they foster and develop patriotic feelings which are later reflected in the rejection of other cultures, religions and ways of life. These children are devoted and loyal, keep their friends and cherish relationships which can later be deranged by excessive expectations. They never enter into relationships superficially and have the need for deep experiences based on the mutual giving. They should be taught from the early age to get rid of unnecessary things, because they develop the collectors' spirit, and it turns out eventually that everything is important or necessary to them. If the excessive possessiveness is noticed, it should be blocked at an innocent age, because later they would become possessive lovers, parents and friends. Their strength is reflected in the family environment, which is supposed to be warm, safe and stable. If in their childhood they get emotionally hurt, it takes them a lot of time to recover and heal their wounds. They are physically pretty strong, but may be of gentler health just because of the seething emotions which burden the psyche, which is later reflected through the poor digestion or slow metabolism. It often happens that they are left with scars from the childhood, which is later projected on their marriage, family relationship or job. These children are capable, practical, creative and introverted. In mature age they are effective in private business, military and government services and sports. They understand the importance of family early, and develop the sense of protectiveness and the instinct when something is wrong at home. It would be good if their parents spared them traumas, disagreements, frictions, or bursts of temper, especially if severe situations happen. If they become the witnesses of family dramas, in the mature age they become especially cruel towards bullies, drunken fathers or unstable people. We should not forget that these children love honestly and gently, they expect a lot of love and are selflessly giving love, so to love them is a blessing and a balm for the soul.

They have developed memory, so they carry things from their childhood deep into the old age. If you treat them well, they will be faithful and loyal to you for life.

## Leo child (sign & ascendant)

These children truly get from the universe the abundance of creative energy and power. Through them we can usually see how the sky is generous, bright and shiny. Through these children we see that a man can achieve everything he wants, and that the entire universe will turn upside down to do what their hearts wish for. Children born in the sign of Leo exhibit the leadership skills at an early age. The insecure children and all those in need of protection and assistance feel good in their company. They early exhibit the patronizing attitude and the need to protect the weak. They are rarely lonely and introverted. They have the need to stand out, to create and they clearly manifest what they want. From the early childhood they are convinced that they are the best and that the others need to listen and follow them. This attitude creates the antagonism, especially in children who are individual, strong and able to live without the "royal leader". In order to prevent the discomfort and conflicts as they grow up, these children need to be explained that the others around them are also special, unique and different in something. They should also be showed that the creative potential they possess represents the divine grace; therefore the same should be treated with great respect. These children often acquire serious and powerful enemies later in life because they are superior in everything. Children born in the sign of Leo win even when there is no solid ground for it, even when they are lower in quality than the other children. Their strength is reflected in generosity, protective relationship (especially towards the girls and delicate children) and the need to share happiness with others. If your child is depressed, dispirited and anxious, feel free to take him to meet little Leos and you will notice the desire to play, have fun, and prove them. The strong ego in children born in the sign of Leo often creates the inconvenient and stubborn character later, so they do not forgive themselves if they serve others, or if they are subordinate in any way. In the adult age they are scorned because they look down on the others. These children rarely do not succeed in life. It is sufficient to say that Napoleon, Caesar, Mussolini, Fidel Castro, Madonna and many others were born in this sign, and there is almost no prime-minister or head of state without the sign of Leo in the Ascendant or in the Sun sign. These children are born to create and share their gifts with others. They are born to give a lot of love and launch, protect and inspire others with their warmth, grace and power. We should never forget that their existence is bound to giving, so from early age selfishness, conceit and pride should be eradicated. If treated properly they can create wonders and build new worlds and systems of values.

## Virgo child (sign & ascendant)

If people could choose for themselves calm, smart and diligent children they would probably want them to be born in the sign of Virgo. They exhibit the excessive maturity and seriousness early, which cannot easily be seen in the other children. They are obedient, calm, gentle and often insecure. They perform their daily duties meticulously and accurately and execute them with much effort, beautification and effort. One should never be severe with these kids, because they are tremendously trying to gain attention, praise, a gentle word, a hug or a compliment. They don't have large appetites, perfectly understand what scarcity and deprivation mean and are easy to rise. If parents in their early childhood show cruelty or strictness, it would take years to heal the scars, raise confidence and correctly form the character. They can be quite timid and worried by nature, so they are often bypassed by the basic and innocent children's joys. They look upon life very seriously and responsibly mostly from the early age, which is a salve for the parents' soul, but for their gentle souls that cannot be good. Certainly, they need to be taught to play more, socialize and relax in the company, because they can express anxiety, suspicion and mistrust. They are not belligerent or rough by nature, do not know how to protect and defend themselves, and therefore are left to the mercy of children who are overly active, violent or forceful. Children born in the sign of Virgo are modest, calm and meticulous; they are rarely vulgar or rarely cause trouble. They finish schooling mostly alone, without the help of parents, with a lot of effort and hard work unlike those born in the sign of Gemini. Children born in the sign of Virgo must be taught to be happy, because to them life goes by in effort, organization and the need to appeal to someone. From the early age their self-confidence should be stimulated, accepting praise and compliments, as well as the awareness that they are equal with others. If the leadership qualities are not woken up in childhood, Virgos as adults refuse managers' positions or are not ready for the progress. The self-sufficient people who are lagging behind in quality often 'squeeze' in their places. Children born in this sign can be left alone at home or entrusted with an important task. They perceive everything seriously, devotedly and responsibly, but are hard to learn happiness and innocent rejoicing. The laugh, dance, play and fun should be stimulated since they often have modest childhood because of their introverted nature, and then later in life remember that they were good at school or at the labor action. They need to be taught that even when we grow up God loves the children in us and the innocent joy that is now so rare to be seen. Such children are a true blessing. Unfortunately, parents often take their uniqueness easily, so they are rigorous and critically-oriented towards them. Rejoice with these children and teach them that life is not only in the lessons we have to learn. There is time for everything, so there is time for relaxation, pleasure and joy.

## *Libra child (sign & ascendant)*

Libra in mythology stands with the goddess Aphrodite who represents love, sensuality and art. Children born in the sign of Libra can be compared to the beautiful, precious vase. The Creator skillfully merged beauty with the form in them. They have the innate manners, strive to beautiful

things, enjoy and connect with others. They express creative skills early, speak nicely, combine colors and images
easily, and dress as dandies in the latest fashion. They have
a heightened awareness of the fact that they have to connect with others, so they exercise comradeship early, and
then relationships and friendships later. They are capable
of maintaining spurious and artificial contacts with everybody, but as much as it may seem strange, their biggest
weaknesses are the relationships with people. They need
to be stimulated to be direct, open, enterprising and courageous, which are the traits which these children certainly
lack. Because of their strange need to fulfill everyone's demands and maintain the positive image, they come home
tired and exhausted. This kind of "fineness" requires a lot
of energy. Libras are not able to be alone so they conclude
the early "alliances", and later in life they cannot function
without a partner or someone who would constantly guide,
support, encourage and cheer them. For this reason, they
make the most difficult emotional contacts and relationships with the closest people, because in the outside world
they hide behind a mask of civility, refinement and good
behavior. When such children are asked: "Would you like
an apple pie or a potato pie?" they respond: "Whichever".
It is hard for them to make decisions because of the need
to harmonize all the relationships, which is almost impossible in real life. Their self-confidence is often under-
mined, so they invest a lot of energy in order to conceal the
indecision and vacillation. They want to fulfill everyone's
wishes, but later suffer criticism from those who have the
highest expectations. They need to learn to develop individuality and independence so as not to expect the support
and confirmation from the others. It is not evident early in
childhood, but later in life, when Libras remain single or
have emotional problems; they need a long time to rebuild
a normal life. These children need to be loved always and
need to give love very early. The emotional relationships
are something they will continually strive to, but there exists the possibility of harm and disappointments. On the
other hand, these kids love to show that the heavens were
generous, and they were rewarded with the lavish talents,

beauty and posture. We can often see that in life they grow into the great artists, singers, dancers, and are always where beauty, enjoyment and creation are. The following people were born in the sign of Libra: Brigitte Bardot, Ivo Pogorelich, Franz Liszt, John Lennon, Bob Geldof, Miguel de Cervantes and many others who left a number of artistic achievements to the world.

## *Scorpio child (sign & ascendant)*

These children can be compared to the moody, restless river, which can pour out of its banks instantly. Their lives are never ordinary and the lessons they learn are never easy. Children Scorpios are born to correct the errors of ancestors and later in life take on them the burden of responsibility for everything that was once upon a time, in the past. They are characterized by the attractive, enigmatic appearance, magnetism and the seduction that comes from the unknown. People are attracted to everything inscrutable and unknown, and Scorpios bear the enormous charisma and the inexhaustible energy which is restored in moments of fatigue, weakness or exhaustion. These children understand the importance of existence on the Earth early; they often turn to strange occupations and have unusual interests. As this is the water, occult sign of the enormous power, the fear of the surprise hides behind, the fear that people and events cannot be controlled, so the suspicion, alertness and possessiveness are born early. They have an innate competitive drive, but it is cleverly hidden and masked, so that the others are often surprised when they realize that the biggest and the most dangerous opponents were the quietest and the inmost persons. A Scorpio should be taught to release the emotions and forget about the insults and emotional injuries. If such a spirit is not tamed in childhood, they become the fanatical followers of their goals, and it becomes great danger to provoke anger or rivalry in them. Once a Scorpio gets hurt, it takes them years to heal the wounds and recover. It would be good for them to keep away from dangerous situations because they cannot leave dramatic spots, despite being visibly excited and anxious. If their parents show cruelty or coldness, they will get the chance to feel the revenge in the years when they show impotence or weakness. Scorpios are wonderful and faithful friends whom you can always rely on. They are loyal, but it is hard for them to forgive betrayal, volatility, abandonment or fickleness. They are capable of pursuing their goals fanatically and there is no sign which can better take the blows of fate, difficult experiences and rubbles in life. They have strong survival instinct, strong intuition, creative potential and wisdom which are not typical of the other signs of the Zodiac. Their trouble is that they experience everything too intensely; they identify with different situations and therefore suffer or become notorious. It rarely happens that a Scorpio is not successful, and it is necessary to detect their talents early, since they're hard to reveal and show. These children often hold within them the things that bother and pervade them, which their parents do not even suspect. Their strength lies in the divine wisdom, the ability to help others and to forgive. If they succeed in it, they become doctors, surgeons, healers and therapists. They have the power to heal others, but before that they must learn to help themselves. People who were born in the sign of Scorpio: Alain Delon, Paganini, Dostoyevsky, Grace Kelly, Maradona, Prince Charles, Picasso, Charles Bronson and many others who have enchanted the world with their charisma, knowledge and creative qualities.

## *Sagittarius child (sign & ascendant)*

Of all the signs of the Zodiac Sagittarius is somehow the darling of the Creator, and we can notice that they enjoy the most happiness, divine grace; they are often spared of the severe, excruciating fate and hard work. Children born in the sign of Sagittarius are good-hearted, cheerful, and full of optimism and the inborn faith. They are rarely depressed and despondent; they know how to be happy, play with other children and use all the benefits that life gives. Some valid and good solution always appears for these children, they are always spared the lessons which other people must learn and they are almost never left alone, forgotten and discarded. Even if a child Sagittarius does something wrong, their parents and friends understand, forgive and tolerate it. If a Sagittarius is weak, in a life crisis or decline, the others always come to the rescue, to heal, venerate and bless. If a child Sagittarius wants something, the Creator will always ensure that his wishes are fulfilled. If a child is born in the sign of Sagittarius then you can be sure that in the family or genetics there were good, hardworking, moral people, so that now it can enjoy all the benefits of life. They rarely lose faith and the life's sense. This kind of optimism can be healing and helpful to the others, but sometimes also fatal, because there are days when life only takes from a man. In those moments, Sagittarius does not cope well because they are accustomed to everything going smoothly and without difficulty. In addition to the strong faith and enthusiasm they have coldness hiding behind the high energy and power. For this reason Sagittarius rarely envies anyone because they are highly self-centered and do not develop the excessive closeness with the others. You'll see that the child Sagittarius is often glad when the others achieve better results, but the inferiority of the others compared to his own life is behind that. They should be showed in the early childhood that energy, faith and courage are best when spent helping others. Unfortunately, each Sagittarius spends his life in hedonism, pleasure and good opportunities. They are often incapable of feeling the suffering of others because they are devoid of serious breakages and complicated life situations. Sagittarius child can travel wherever he/she wants. He is the darling of God and money from an early age. It is not wrong that these children rejoice and enjoy, the trouble is that when they are middle-aged they exaggerate in everything, and spend life in eating, drinking and spending money. It should be understood that each of us is born for a higher purpose and that a man helps himself by healing and saving others. Sagittarius can become great Teachers only if they develop faith, morality and love for others in the right time. Beethoven, Frank

Sinatra, Winston Churchill, Maria Callas, Edith Piaf, Leonid Brezhnev, Mark Twain, Alberto Moravia and many others were born in the sign of Sagittarius.

# Capricorn child (sign & ascendant)

Unlike children born in the sign of Sagittarius, Capricorns do not have such easy and carefree life, nor do they grow up wrapped in silk and velvet. They are very smart children who learn very early about actual materialistic values of this world and early realize that a man is worth as much as he does or acquires in life. Capricorn is the most ambitious of all signs and most enduring to carry out his wishes in practice. Due to this reason, children Capricorns early become concrete, practical and materialistic. From the early age they learn how to make two out of one dollar and see in everything the possibilities to provide for themselves later in life. If in the horoscopes of these children there are other earth elements (Taurus and Virgo) they tend to the materialistic things from the early age, which is later reflected in the spiritual poverty, blindness with money and recognition. Although many people think that Leo and the like lead the world, in the end we are somehow assured that Capricorns get the most, because they create for years and have the patience to wait what they have planted in their childhood or the early youth. If in the childhood they understood that money, achievements and success are not everything in life, these children become mature, responsible and diligent people, ready to start a family. The influence of the traditional values should be mitigated in a way, because later it is very important to them what the environment thinks and how people look at some of their problems. For this reason you can see that in mature age they are not able to finish bad relationships, but persist in bad marriages, relationships or cold family life. They solve their problems by living double lives, and people still say that their marriage is good and harmonious. It is also important that these children feel the closeness of their parents. It would be desirable that the parents get along well, exchange tenderness and tolerance, so that their children could one day enjoy a good family life. Like Cancer, a Capricorn also prefers everything which is homemade, and it sometimes gets to the extreme. For this reason, these children learn to respect diversity and difference. It takes a lot of time for a Capricorn to accept and understand something, so if they create rigid attitudes in their childhood, it will hardly be corrected or healed by somebody later. These children are often taught that everything old, archaic and long gone is good, so in modern times they have problems to develop and progress. They are obedient and committed, so in childhood they already become good workers willing to make sacrifices, ready for difficult life conditions, they do not complain about poverty, scarcity and dearth, which is a relief for their parents. It is necessary to lessen the development of critical thinking within them and cherish the romantic and tender feelings. Their weaknesses are emotions, so that it happens that Capricorns are not the image of the warmest and the most vulnerable people. This is certainly treated in the early childhood with love, care and dedication. The following people were born in the sign of Capricorn: Stalin, Frederico Fellini, Johannes Kepler, Al Capone, Richard Nixon, Mao Tse Dung, David Bowie, Isaac Newton and many others.

## *Aquarius child (sign & ascendant)*

In his creative rapture Creator specifically addressed Aquarius allowing them to understand, see and think faster and better than other people. There is no sign which can match him, nor intellectually compete with him. Children Aquarians are often tall (especially with the Ascendant in Aquarius), unusual and free in the appearance and behavior. Such children do not like chains, clamps and shackles, choose their paths themselves, being unique, inimitable and rebellious which causes great difficulties later in life. In the early childhood they show strong resistance to based patterns, entrenched beliefs, having difficulties to understand traditionalists, slow thinkers and those who do not express themselves easily. Child Aquarius likes to choose his own path, even if this journey is uncomfortable and unpleasant. They enjoy growing in families which understand their needs and rejoice if the others approve of their attitudes. Such children are first to accept the things which are inexplicable, illogical and absurd to others. They enjoy supporting people who are rejected, lonely or strange in some way. They are always where the progress, the evolution, new concepts or ideas are. They are able to get far ahead of the other children and it is difficult for them to understand why the others are so far behind. Although the astrological texts often mention that the geniuses are born in this sign, it mustn't be forgotten that they are musical, mystical, with the deep sense of justice, equality and equity. They are capable of losing everything they have if they believe they follow the right goal and that they make sacrifice because of someone. Although they have the capricious nature, these children are rarely alone, but few people know that they are really very lonely. If they're not treated with care and patience they later grow to be weirdoes, loners and eccentrics. People often think that Leos are egotistical, but we can see Leos who serve or cheer their rivals and competitors, however, the true egocentrism is reflected in an Aquarius who is neither able to admire anybody, nor to follow someone. From such a trouble many others are born, and later in life we see that Aquarians have bad relationships with parents and the authorities, often are divorced or without a real life companion. As much as they are capable of fighting for the rights of others, an Aquarius finds it difficult to establish intimacy with one person. From the early age they should be taught the beauty of admiration and respect for others, as well as the development of feelings which can be suppressed. The following people were born in the sign of Aquarius: Bob Marley, Phil Collins, Edgar Monet, Nastassia Kinski, John Travolta, Adler, Clark Gable, Schubert, Darwin, Galileo, Edison, Stendal, Byron, Mozart, Jules Verne, James Joyce, Byron, James Dean, Artur Rubinstein, Paul Newman, Charles Dickens and many others.

## *Pisces child (sign & ascendant)*

Astrologers believe that the people born in the sign of Pisces were imposed the toughest task in which they should comprehend the human suffering, destruction, grief and understand why a man passes difficult and unusual challenges during the life's journey. Pisces are born hypersensitive, emotional, disguised and concealed; it is often difficult to determine what is really happening in their little souls. As much as the signs of the Zodiac are known to a man and the astrologers, the truth is that the least is known of Pisces. These children often grow tall; they're inclined to weight gain, fantasies, isolation and withdrawal. They are imaginative, passive, friendly, reckless and prone to delusions. For this reason, they often "pull out the short end", suffer unfairly or are embroiled in nasty situations because of the others. They are the easiest to manipulate, so it is necessary to follow the development patiently, the environment in which they grow up and not allow them to interfere with the troubled, aggressive or moody children. Since they are gullible, quiet and insecure, it is easy to get them into trouble and play around with them. If they are not hardened from the early age, it later leads both them and the others into problems. It is important to develop decisiveness, directness, and sharp observations in them and to teach them that they are not responsible for the fact that the world is made up of light and dark, and therefore, they are not responsible because there are the sick, weak and poor people. Pisces often think they need to take greater burden and that the others' burden is their burden too, which later in life turns out to be naivety, lightheadedness and the excessive compassion. These children are perfect for manipulators and those who play with the human frailties. Due to the excessively strong imagination, hypersensitive and psychic channels they grow into amazing artists, talented musicians, doctors and healers. If parents do not recognize volatility and enchantment in them, they early start living in the world of deception, illusion and mystery, which results in the false creation of the world, non-acceptance of the reality and the impracticality. We often see that in mature years they wander from one to another situation, totally unprepared for all that surrounds them. They should not be encouraged to laziness, bad habits and retreating into the world of isolation. They carry the disappointments experienced in the childhood long in the mature age, and then find solutions to the simple and mundane life lessons in the painful and difficult ways. Their strength lies in their talents, strong impressions and deep consideration of the complexities of life. These kids are good friends, willing to help and support children who are for some reason hurt and withdrawn. They are unselfish, careful and moderate. They rarely become violent, rowdy and rough. It is necessary to develop the courage and strength so that they would later tackle all the things that make life more easily. The following people were born in the sign of Pisces: Johann Strauss, Handel, Chopin, Anna Magnani, Elizabeth Taylor, George Harrison, Victor Hugo, Einstein, Ursula Anders, Liza Minnelli and many others.

*Note: these are just some of the characteristics of the signs of the Zodiac on the basis of which the natal horoscope cannot be interpreted, love and life expectancy assessed or anything alike. Astrology is much more than that. There is a way in which the natal horoscope is connected into a coherent whole. It is clear that not all Aries are brave nor all Cancers emotional and sensitive; therefore, we are talking about the Zodiac signs that possess certain qualities. It is important to understand that certain texts cannot be generalized nor the specific truths and statements established on their basis.*

# Signs of the Zodiac from the perspective of Indian astrology - Jyotish

The Indian astrology is specific due to the fact that it has not changed for thousands of years. In India the science in astrology is marked as Jyotish, which means light. In recent years Jyotish has been especially popular in Europe. There are many differences between the Western and Jyotish astrology. Astrology known to us uses the benefits of the tropic Zodiac (related to the seasons), and the Indian astrology uses the sidereal Zodiac related to the fixed stars, so it can freely be called the "sidereal Zodiac." Over time, a big difference was made between the tropical and sidereal Zodiac, which is called Ajanamsha and today it amounts to about 24 degrees. The result is that both the planets and the Ascendant shift 24 degrees backwards. For example, if the Mercury was located on the second degree of Virgo in the Western system, it would automatically, according to the Vedic system, take a position in the constellation of Leo on Magha (Regulus) nakshatra which is often wise, morose, but gives great success, deep insights and sometimes fame. Still, the whole thing about these two systems is much more complex than you can imagine.

## Aries (Mesa)

Aries is ruled by the planet Mars (Mangal).

Everything which is related to Aries is young, "green" and inexperienced. There is a strong desire to explore, experience and experiment. The masters of Jyotish believe that this soul is young and that in previous incarnations it did not experience anything significant or difficult. If your Ascendant is found on the first degrees of Aries, you can expect success on the material level, prosperity and happiness. Also, the first decade of Aries speaks of courage, intelligence, skill, ingenuity and entrepreneurship.

The second decade of the sign of Aries is somewhat lower, so it speaks about the people who are gentle, indulgent, generous, and ready to help, nurture and protect the others. That part is related to the progress and welfare but with less struggle and stress. It also speaks about richness that comes in the mature age. There is the emphasized feeling for all those persons that are close or family. Therefore, a person needs to take care of someone or to sacrifice for the loved ones in some way. The last degrees of Aries are slightly rougher and more aggressive. If you have the Ascendant or a planet (graha) there, it may happen that you would be impatient, tactless, hasty and abrupt. Also, the risks of injury and unpleasant situations are possible. Either way, a person is born as bold, direct, sharp, capable of great deeds and accomplishments, as well as coping with difficult life lessons and the victory over the much stronger enemy. Aries by the rule has good health; good posture and is not afraid to be proactive in dealing with everything that life brings.

## *Taurus (Vrsabha)*

Taurus is under the rule of Venus (Venus - Shukra), and there is an exalted (elated) Rahu (North Node) in it. Similar to Western astrology Taurus tends to harmony and sensual happiness. However, unlike Western astrology, Taurus in Jyotish does not have as many sensitive places speaking of the atypical sexual preferences (the first and ultimate degree of Taurus including the fixed star Algol and the Pleiades). So, in Jyotish Taurus is sensual, happy and inclined to well-being. He represents the face of the space being, so he is connected to the nose, eyes and ears. He is balanced, striving to harmonious relations, durable, businesslike, artistic, attractive, romantic, sentimental, holds to the past, tends to appropriation, productive, strong, with good memory and a developed sense of beauty.

The first degrees of Taurus are somewhat more aggressive, tougher, aspire to control, so if some planet is found there, a man gets courage, self-confidence, leadership skills and the managerial power.

The second part of Taurus (each sign contains thirty degrees) is much more comfortable and cozy. If the Ascendant or some planets are found in this section, a person shall strive to acquire material goods, enjoyment, buying luxury things... This is quite passionate and sexual part of the Taurus, so it gives good lovers, hedonists, rich people, artists, dreamers and playboys.

The last part of Taurus gives great travelers, explorers, priests, God-seekers. If the Ascendant or the planets (Grahe) are found there, a person will be fine, calm and poised. He/she will avoid problems and troubles and will be remembered as gentle, affectionate and good-natured.

## Gemini (Mithuna)

Gemini is the sign which is under the influence of the planet Mercury (Budh), and Gemini people are somewhat different from what we know of Gemini in the Western astrology. If you know that you have Cancer in the Ascendant, it is likely that from the perspective of Indian astrology your Ascendant is in Gemini (unless it is not about the last six degrees of Cancer). Gemini by Jyotish corresponds to the neck, arms and shoulders. Gemini people are the flexible part of the universe which is especially emphasized by the desire for change, an active mind and motion. Indians believe that Gemini people have the following characteristics: spokesman, poet, traveler, writer, technician, programmer, wish to adopt new information, strong sexual desire, anxiety, impulsivity, divorces several times, varying moods, sensitive, neurotic, dangerous when attached to someone, inclined to strange reactions, unreliable and erratic. They suffer from the pulmonary problems (bronchitis, asthma, tuberculosis...), nervous disorders and cardiovascular problems. There is also a belief that they are prone to injuries and hazards.

If your Ascendant is found in the first five degrees of Gemini, there is a high probability that you will inherit a good, quiet and demure nature which can suffer from insecurity and anxiety. Numerous acquaintances and travels are also possible.

The second part (up to the twentieth degree) is characterized by the rash and restless nature, strong-willed, with the high goals and aspirations. It may happen that a person is followed by numerous conflicts, dangers and strange situations. This part of Gemini is particularly nimble, agile, dexterous and prone to sudden changes. Also, it is characterized by the irrational behavior, disappointments, heavy thoughts and destructiveness. The last degrees of Gemini (each sign has thirty degrees) is characterized by peace, tranquility, good thoughts and vibrations, enthusiasm, strong and deep emotions, empathy, humility, knowledge, spirituality, knowledge of foreign languages, emphasized intuition and wisdom.

## *Cancer (Karka)*

Cancer is ruled by Chandra (Moon), and therefore Jyotish (Indian astrologers) say that he is emotional, changeable, sensitive, prone to sudden changes in mood, receptive, sociable, shares his meal with the others, attaching and seeking attention. Most people, who according to the Western astrology have the Ascendant in Leo, correspond to Cancer in the Indian astrology (unless it is not about the last six degrees of Leo). The Indian astrologers also believe that Cancer rules the heart, lungs and thorax. These people are said to be likable, under the strong influence of family (especially mother), ready to help, share experiences and feelings. They are often loved, achieve success in business and politics, they tend to connect with others (which are quite different from the Cancer we know in the Western astrology). He gains popularity during the lifetime and cares about success, but it happens that he is not too daring, he is under the influence of other people, often a slave to tradition and has to spend the great part of his life in the country where he was born. People see him as open, intuitive, desirous of companionship.

The first degrees of Cancer are quite sensitive and vulnerable, so we can talk about the gentle nature if the Ascendant or a planet finds itself there. That part of Cancer is not problematic at all. People are able to adapt and they develop a good character, calm and polite behavior. If the Ascendant or a planet is found there, a person can attain wisdom, knowledge and certain skills to apply through life. Good luck, success and prosperity follow him. He rarely encounters insurmountable obstacles; the others help or save him from unpleasant situations. He is not inclined to crime, or to the things that can tarnish his reputation.

The central part of Cancer (up to fifteen degrees) also provides a quiet person, a philanthropist inclined to travel and thinking. There is the possibility of acquiring great wealth if the planets (grahas) find themselves there. This part is more positive than the previous one, and the person is favored, loved and respected.

Last parts of Cancer (from the sixteenth to the thirtieth degree) identify themselves with the coiled snake. Instead of the great sex, magic and regenerative power, there is the unnatural jealousy, lust and passion, sexual deviations, sudden environmental changes and stress, breakages and falls, possible dangers and encounters with strange people. If the Ascendant or a planet finds itself there, a person often changes professions, place of residence... The same part of the Cancer is linked to the ability to adapt to the most difficult conditions of life and transformations. If a person is diligent and responsible, he/she acquires vast knowledge and wisdom as well as the special powers (sidhi) to use in life. For some reason a person can be misunderstood and unaccepted by others, but eventually triumphs as a winner. In any case, this is a strange character that breaks the daily norm of behavior.

## Leo (Simha)

Leo is ruled by the Sun (Surya) and it rules the digestive tract, stomach and liver. Most people who in the Western astrology have the Ascendant in Virgo correspond to Leo in the Indian astrology (unless it is about the last six degrees of Virgo). We are talking about the people who have the emphasized need to create, material achievement, success in public, recognition, acquiring reputation and strong social positions. These are people of fine manners, intelligent, hardworking and dedicated to the realization of their desires. It happens that they do not have much luck in love or with children. Fortune or misfortune in the Indian astrology is not measured by whether a person has two or three children, but whether a man gets along well with his children and whether they are a source of suffering and disappointment. Quantity in Jyotish is not the relevant measure of luck. For example, in the Western world a man feels good if he's married and has two mistresses. People from the side see it as a feat, while in the East such behavior is treated as a source of pain and suffering to the family and the women involved in such a love story. So, it is about the different philosophical approach to life in general. Although pretty strong, Leos often suffer from stomach and heart problems, obesity and arthritis.

The first ten degrees of Leo are considered to be particularly important due to the fixed star Regulus, which is always in the same place, as opposed to the Western astrology where it stood for a long time on the twenty-ninth degree of Leo, and now covers the prime degree of Virgo. That part of Leo gives something special and royal. A person may not necessarily be crowned nor be a relative of Prince Charles, but in a lifetime achieves much more than the environment or the other family members. So, we are here talking about the glamour, wealth, luxury, achievements, strong connections, high social lounges. If these planets (grahas) find themselves here or the Ascendant (lagna), a person gets the best qualities from the family, artistic potential... If there were immoral people, liars and thieves in the family, the person falls under the burden of what the ancestry did in the past.

The second part of Leo (up to the twenty-sixth degree) is also artistic, but less militant and less productive. A person is favored, talented, often lazy, passive and inert to do anything. Mostly, things come to him/her without much effort. If, for example, the planet (graha) which governs the field of marriage, finds itself there, your partner could be good looking, enjoys splendor and opulence, but does not like to work, wash dishes, chop wood... And the interpretation in the other segments of life is also similar.

Last degrees of Leo are completely different. We're talking here about prominent intellectual abilities, knowledge, person helping others, the ego is not as emphasized, and there is a desire to serve. A person is calm, calculated, cold and sober. In some cases we get introverted and enigmatic people who have a rich inner life.

## Virgo (Kanya)

Virgo is ruled by Mercury (Budh). It is characterized by good memory, he/she distinguishes details excellently, and he/she is prone to analysis and digression, and sometimes heavy, dark thoughts. It governs the lower part of the digestive tract and hips. Most of the people with the Ascendant in Libra, according to the Western astrology, correspond to Virgo (Kanya) in the Indian astrology (unless it is about the last six degrees of Libra). The Indian astrology says that Virgos are anxious, intellectual, nervous, tense, and sensitive to the external stimuli... We can find them in medicine (doctors, healers, caregivers...), but we also meet them as actors, artists, craftsmen, teachers and lecturers. Virgos are particularly practical, rational, with the expressed intellect, conscientious and responsible. They are of gentle health. They suffer from bloating, constipation, hernia, nerve diseases... Sometimes it happens that the strange and insidious diseases haunt them, such as multiple sclerosis and Parkinsonism. It would be good for them to eat a variety of spices, carrots, variety of fruits and vegetables.

The first ten degrees of Virgo are ruled by the Sun (Surya) and they influence the work of the genitals. This is the intellectual part of Virgo, and if the Ascendant or the planets find themselves there, we can find teachers, intellectuals, priests, and humble people able to serve, listen to others and help them. The talent for writing, learning foreign languages and philosophy can also be developed. This part of Virgo is particularly quiet, and there is no question of aggression, violent, theatrical behavior or strong self-awareness.

The second part (which extends to the twenty-third degree of Virgo) is a lot stronger, more stable and more concrete. We're not talking about serving here. These are people who struggle, work hard, overcome obstacles, get to grips with the life's challenges; they are able to adapt and get what they want. Sometimes they can be found in politics, the financial system or militaristic services. There is a desire for the imposition of the will and control. This is the vital part of Virgo. If the planets (grahas) or the Ascendant (lagna) find themselves there, a person recovers quickly from illnesses. Over time, the character changes, so these people can become dishonest or difficult.

The last six degrees of Virgo give a pretty face, wealth, abundance, good opportunities, strong sexuality, sensuality and attractiveness, as well as the ability to take advantage of practical values of life. These people build their lives, stone by stone, but without the excessive struggle and effort.

## *Libra (Tula)*

When we talk about Libra in the Western astrology, the astrologer often, due to the lack of imagination, first thinks of a porcelain vase, beautiful furniture, comfort and manners, which is somewhat true, but far from the truth. In the Indian astrology Libra (Tula) has a slightly different meaning.

Libra is ruled by Venus (Shukra) and should possess a refined taste for harmony and beauty. Unlike the Western astrology, in which Libra begs and prays for a little attention and fails to keep up in the material world by herself and without a partner, in the Indian astrology, she longs for fame, recognition, leadership and achievement. Those better informed will understand that this is about Scorpios, looking from the perspective of the Western astrology. They say that Libra (Tula) governs the urinary tract, reproductive organs (especially female) and kidneys. Jyotish also believe that people born in the sign of Libra are leaders, rebels, revolutionaries, trying to create balance in relationships, hence resulting in problems, conflicts and misunderstandings. They are capable of seeing and feeling beauty in many things, they go through life full of ideas and idealism, able to understand the social events, happenings in the world... They say they have the incredible feeling for people, understand the needs of society and can influence the masses. In addition, they do not feel the excessive need for home and family, so they get married later or think about having kids later. They are fanatical in everything they do, they expect loyalty and affection from the others, which is difficult to achieve in practice, partly because the human being is mired in the material. Libra seeks audience and stage, so they do not like to work in the shadows and try to be noticed as much as possible. They succeed in life, but with numerous conflicts, fights, settling old scores and severe emotional injuries. If Venus (Shukra) is badly placed at the time of birth, it is necessary to fast on Fridays. Libras are usually healthy, if they control the intake of sugar. They get seriously sick, mainly due to bad habits, stress and the excessive effort. They should avoid alcoholic drinks, white sugar and flour. It is advisable to wear clothes made of cotton and silk.

The first seven degrees of Libra (Spike) are ruled by Mars (Mangal). This is about the attractive, charismatic and attractive people who love the stage, shine and splendor. It is believed that they have artistic inclinations, talents, and the emphasized sense of justice and beauty. Sometimes they are speakers, writers, diplomats, actors...

The second part of Libra (up to the twentieth degree, Arcturus) is under the rule of the northern node (Rahu). Here are frequent moves, stress, strong and disturbing changes, home drama, these people often start from scratch, and they climb and fall. This is about fighters, winners, and all who do not shy away from the challenges of life but tolerate fractures, turbulence and challenges well. These people are craving for success, and sometimes do not hesitate just to reach the desired goal. In these parts of Libra the self-confidence and motivation are emphasized, but also the support from the other people. Although these people are sharp and combative, they are often hypersensitive but they hide that from the others skillfully. This can mean a lifetime on the move or on the wheels.

The last degrees of Libra (Kiffa Australis) are ruled by Guru (Jupiter). These people are completely individual and there is no chance for teamwork. They go from one extreme to another, so they may be particularly good or the extremely bad guys. They succeed in life disregarding obstacles and challenges. There is no need to worry about them because they are goal and success oriented from the early age.

## Scorpio (Vrscika)

Scorpio (Vrscika) is ruled by Mars (Mangal). It has the unusual energy which is different from the other signs. They are very enthusiastic, dynamic, energetic, and full of strength, determination and entrepreneurial spirit. Indian astrologers (Jyotish) believe that Scorpio governs the genitals. Scorpios are born explorers, deep and intense, so they are found in all areas of the art (poets, storytellers, satirists, essayists and pamphleteers, actors...), and we also meet them in medicine (surgeons, pathologists, and gynecologists), the spheres of spirituality and esoteria (astrologers, yoga instructors, practitioners of magic, Kabbalists...). Also, they have the urge to show their strength, stamina, endurance and power, so we find them in the police, military, and sports. Scorpios are of medium height, muscular and often hairy... they are intensive in sex, martial arts, they fall into conflicts and it is difficult for them to control themselves. They are full of self-confidence, stubborn, sharp and uncompromising. They can be quite aggressive and violent if they feel threatened. If the planet Mars (Mangal) is damaged, it would be advisable to fast on Tuesdays. They often suffer from allergies, diseases of the liver and venereal diseases. They should avoid food with lots of protein, stimulants, dishes that arouse senses, spicy food, and alcohol.

The first half of the Scorpio (from the third to the six-teenth degree, Izidis) is ruled by Saturn (Shani) and can give good-natured persons, sociable, friendly, spiritual, meek and directed towards the other people. If the planets (grahas) or the Ascendant (lagna) find themselves there, a person may taste significant and profound love experiences.

The second part of the Scorpio (from the sixteenth to the thirtieth degree, Antares) is ruled by Mercury (Budh). Here we talk about people who have special powers or techniques to achieve remarkable things in life. Beneath the calm exterior hides the brave and warrior heart. Planets (grahas) placed in this section highlight the spiritual and healing powers.

## Sagittarius (Dhanusa)

Sagittarius (Dhanusa) is ruled by Jupiter (Guru), and it is adorned by very strong moral, religious and spiritual principles. It possesses the groundless optimism, positive attitude towards life and its laws, and it is often accompanied by luck and favorable circumstances. Masters of the Indian astrology believe that Sagittarius (Dhanusa) governs the thighs and hips. A Sagittarius is honorable, honest, courageous, responsible, moral, seeks perfection and complete harmony. He is good-natured, loyal, believes in miracles and goodness, so he is often suckered, ridiculed and fooled. A Sagittarius is tall, athletic, and narrow shouldered, with wide hips and strong, pronounced jaw. In his mind everything is simple, honest and beautiful, life is beautiful, and happiness is achieved without the hassle and fuss. In this he may be envied by every other sign. A Sagittarius is righteous to him and others, forgives infidelity, betrayal, puts up with the misanthropes, and easily forgets insults. In his lifetime he is followed by moving, turbulent events and numerous acquaintances. A Sagittarius sometimes suffers from diabetes, high cholesterol, and obesity. It would be advisable to wear clothes in orange and yellow, and occasionally fast on Thursdays.

The first part of Sagittarius (to the fourteenth degree, Saul) is ruled by the southern node (Kato) and is particularly demanding. Only a few have enough strength and courage to bear the burden of life. This part of Sagittarius can be characterized by the verses of the Lebanese poet Khalil Gibran: "There is much in you but a man, a lot more is not a man, but a formless dwarf who go in a dream through the fog looking for his own awakening."

If the Ascendant (lagna) or planets (grahas) find themselves there, a person can express the primitive animalistic part of the personality which aspires to achievements, material pleasures. Because of this approach to life he can fall to the bottom and experience great loss. The second part of the story is related to the special spiritual accomplishments that allow a man to communicate with God and the higher beings. Hardly anyone actually manages to live the other part of the story, but it comes down to business success and the sudden collapse from the throne.

The second part of Sagittarius (up to the twenty sixth degrees, Ascela) is ruled by Venus (Shukra). Here it is about the good, reasonable, fine and peaceful people who achieve a lot, thanks to the positive attitude and faith in God. This part of Sagittarius is more calm and stable.

The last degrees of the sign (Kaus Medius) are ruled by the Sun (Surya), and here we can speak of brave, famous, influential and successful people who are aggressive in the material, and the spiritual realization. They are capable, skilled, wise and skillful. These people go through life with the pure heart.

## Capricorn (Makara)

Capricorn is ruled by Saturn (Shani). It is believed that he strives to the power, ambition, achievement and every kind of material security. It is well organized, respects order and tradition, rarely found in the eccentric situations and unconventional relationships. Capricorn (Makara) aspires to realization in the outer, visible and tangible world, while for the inner, esoteric and spiritual, he almost does not care. Jyotish believe that Capricorn rules joints and bones. He suffers from arthritis, ligaments weakness and osteoporosis. They are also not immune to stress, however, they often suffer from heart problems and high blood pressure. If Shani (Saturn) is poorly placed in the chart, it is difficult to recover after the illness or stressful life lessons. It would be desirable to fast on Saturdays (it involves only the use of fruits and vegetables), wear black clothes, and in any way help the old people, cripples and those alienated and rejected from society. It is also good to stimulate the workplace or home by blue sapphire, as well as the specific, strong scents that neutralize negative forces and induce positive energy.

A Capricorn is practical, frugal, good worker and even better organizer of his own and other people's time. He often encounters numerous obstacles to achieving his goals. The road is always bumpy, but a Capricorn is capable of the long-term success and well withstands the hardships and the blows of fate.

The first ten degrees of Capricorn (Kaus Medius) is under the reign of the Sun (Surya) and it is about the sharp, intelligent and peaceful person who is able to make a lot out of little. He/she abounds in self-confidence, wisdom and the need for order. It often happens that he/she possesses the artistic talents or a special gift she inherited from the ancestors.

The second part (up to the twenty-third degree, Altair) is ruled by the Moon (Chandra). If the Ascendant (lagna) or the planets (grahas) find themselves there, a person can be famous, successful and rich. Also, the psychic abilities, the ability for the spiritual growth and progress are attributed to them. With this position we find healers, shamans and psychologists. A person comes to success by the hard work, effort and dedication. In the lifetime he/she can repeatedly be deceived, the enemies can appear even in the form of parents, guardians, relatives and all those who behave in a protective way. A person is prone to secret knowledge, learns well and eventually becomes wise and prudent.

The last few degrees of Capricorn (Delphinus) are under the rule of Mars (Mangal). In this case the person is courageous, combative, abrupt, uncompromising and fearless. Jyotish believe that this part is the happiest of all; these people achieve outstanding results in all areas of life. They are also convinced that those are the fortunate persons wherever they go, favored in dangerous situations and capable of protecting themselves and others. These people often achieve a lot more above the expectations.

## Aquarius (Kumbha)

Aquarius (Kumbha) is ruled by Saturn (Shani). Like in the Western astrology, selflessness, ability to sacrifice for other people or ideals is attributed to them. Aquarius is capable of fighting for higher goals and looks at things broadly. So, it is interested in the welfare of the community and society and it subordinates all of the personal aspirations to the collective or to the groups. There is no need to explain that because of this attitude they often "get the worst of it" and become victims of the humanistic worldview. Aquarius is ready to serve if there is a good reason or life belief. All their life they try to understand the others, and it moves them away from self-knowledge. Because of the need to infiltrate into the society, they often miss their private lives, and cause much damage to themselves and the closest people. Jyotish believe that Aquarius governs shins and that for lifetime they fail to develop true individuality, even though they try to do everything "on their own". Freedom, sexual deviations, lack of charisma and proper judgment are attributed to them, and they suffer accusations that they are cold, calculating and reserved from the most beloved. Jyotish say Aquarians suffer from indigestion, skin and lung diseases.

The first seven degrees of Aquarius (Delphinus) are ruled by Mars (Mangal). Here we are free to talk about the brave, eccentric and original person, whether there are found the Ascendant (lagna) or the planets (grahas). Jyotish believe that these people turn all into the triumph and the venture, regardless of which area of life it was. This part is related to talents, creative abilities, emphasized hearing and musicality.

The second part of Aquarius (to the twentieth degree) is ruled by the northern node (Rahu). In this case we find people who are dedicated, quiet, esoteric and spiritual. They are not particularly eager to society. They aspire to isolation, seclusion, prayer and fasting. If the planets (grahas) are found there, a person should spend plenty of time as an ascetic, consciously alienated from the world. The Indian astrologers claim that these people have special healing powers, and all sorts of miraculous powers. These people should be treated nicely and a lot of tenderness and warmth should be given to them. They are able to understand the human suffering and weaknesses.

The last ten degrees of Aquarius (Makrab) are ruled by Jupiter (Guru). They say that these people can be sudden, harsh, unpleasant and of the variable behavior. In life they pass tough and serious lessons, they often face the obstacles, restrictions and hostility. Nothing goes smoothly and everything demands the great effort. It happens that these people are pessimistic, prone to heavy thoughts, brooding and self-destructiveness. Their lives are filled with all sorts of insurmountable obstacles, traps and they arrive to their destination through all sorts of mazes. If they endure hardships and limitations, they rise up and become really great personalities.

## Pisces (Mina)

Pisces are ruled by Jupiter (Guru) and the Indian astrologers believe that these are the gentle, indulgent, changing and insecure people. The following characteristics are also attributed to them: bad leaders, lack of confidence, impractical, abstract, compassionate, artistic, dreamy, full of secrets, curious, imaginative, hidden, happy to sacrifice, capable of deception are often themselves deceived, not too wise, or so deep, intuitive and full of enthusiasm, are dependent on others (particularly partners), but the others also become addicted to them. Their weakness is reflected in the emotional blockages that they hide from the others, and they idealize Pisces that are gentle and criticize those who are seemingly cold and restrained. It happens that people are often not right and get hurt by Pisces who are supposedly merciful, and experience the great good fortune of those who acted cold and reserved.

Pisces suffer from skin diseases, diabetes and emotional problems. Heart problems and indigestion also occur in the middle age.

The first three degrees of Pisces (Moccarabia) is ruled by Jupiter (Guru), and it is assumed that these people are practical, capable, good-hearted, lukewarm, if not provoked or drawn into the problem. Then they can express their coldness, cruelty and sharpness. For some reason, they are prone to problems, or can be drawn into danger (if there are planets or the Ascendant there). It is also possible that these people are forced to taste the difficult life lessons, combat and customization.

The second part of Pisces (to the seventeenth degree) is ruled by Saturn (Shani). This part is slightly happier and easier for life, so we find that planets (grahas) in this part provide talented people, full of creativity and creative power. Power, strength and endurance adorn the people with the Ascendant (lagna) there.

The rest of Pisces is ruled by Mercury (Budh). Here we can rightfully speak of the intuition, emphasized kindness, spirituality, important life experiences, travels, discoveries and the need to help and serve the others. This is an especially spiritual part of Pisces.

# HOUSES IN HOROSCOPE
# AND THEIR SIGNIFICANCE

**Horoscope** houses are particularly significant because they indicate where the energy is directed and in which fields (areas) our life takes place. For example, someone has the fourth house of the horoscope emphasized, and therefore, he is particularly fond of family and parents, and another has the eleventh, but in his nature there is the need for socializing, meeting people and gaining new experiences. For each of us there is a specific plan and a different one for each. What we, as active participants in *the Plan*, have to do is to understand better our own possibilities and understand where our attention is concentrated. The houses of the Zodiac show where *the Plan* is developed and implemented (abroad, work, office, family environment, a neighboring town...) and they are very useful for the interpretation of the natal horoscope. On this occasion, we will briefly describe the houses of the horoscope and their meaning.

> *Certainly, there are those, who besides love, think about how to feed their families, how to provide the fuel and stay healthy in the cramped times. Certainly, there are those who do not resort to drugs, anxiety, fears and all sorts of stimuli that make life look better and time done more easily. Certainly, there are people who must save this crazy world, because not everyone can be drunk and on medications.*

> *Somebody has to heal and help others. Not everyone can be poor and sick. Someone has to stand up straight like a tree. Someone has to bear the burden of this world on his shoulders.*

> Leo Daniel (Daniel Sijakovic)

**The first house** of the horoscope is particularly important because it speaks about the temperament, personality, physical appearance (body, life energy, health) and predispositions of the Natus (the born one) received by birth. Many planets in the first field epitomize a person who is focused on the self and has a strong ego, but also describe the Natus that is difficult to control, hard to be manipulated and advised. Lots of good planets (benefics) in the first field give a solid character and a lot of luck in life, while the poor (malefic) planets could indicate a difficult and inconvenient character, disabilities, illnesses and other problems. So, the person with the Moon in the first house can be of gentle health, unsteady and sensitive, popular and favorite among women, with a pretty face, while the Sun in the first house will talk about a strong individual, strong consciousness, selfishness and egocentrism. The Sun in this position could give a very good health or accelerate the recovery, if the Natus fell sick. Planet Mars in the first field could give a lot of energy, hairiness, dark hair, pronounced nose, fighting spirit, and in its bad aspects the unpleasant character or physical injuries. For a clearer picture we need to assess Mars in the sign and in aspects, as well as the position of its dispositor. Venus in the first house can give the Natus good looks, easy gains, talents, tendency towards art and love of delights. Saturn in the first house gives a rigorous and slow character, skeptical, precocious person, a victim of duty and a pessimistic attitude towards life. Mercury in the first house is about youthful people, travelers, intellectuals or people who live of their words. Also, we cannot banalize astrology and it is necessary to consider other factors in the horoscope carefully. Uranus in the first field brings originality and nervousness, unusual character, a tendency toward the same sex, talent, and Pluto gives fears, the ability to mastermind the others, the gift for technical sciences, while Neptune creates the need for escaping from reality and aspiration to vices, hypersensitivity and special creative abilities (music, writing, painting, intuitiveness, accentuated dreamy character...).

*Not everyone is born to be rich. To be rich or well-known, you have to be ready for it. Today one gets a raise and does not know what to do with it, then goes harassing everyone.*

*We are often only the observers of somebody's wealth and happiness. We can talk about it over a cup of coffee, since we are fed up with watching.*

*Leo Daniel (Daniel Sijakovic)*

**The second house** in the horoscope is extremely important because it speaks about our talents for getting and keeping money. It talks about our money, movable property and describes financial possibilities. It shows the way in which food, substance or money circulates throughout our lives (what we like to eat, how we spend, if we have increased appetite, the way food affects our vitality...). It is extremely important in which sign the second house starts, and, say, its peak in Capricorn indicates slower earnings or gains later in life, money from politics, while Aries on top of the second house is about spending money easily. A lot of good planets in the second house indicate a potential wealth and possibility that the person is financially secured, while malefic planets indicate poverty, misery, renunciation, hunger, acquisition with effort or gains later in life. Some astrologers believe that the second house is also the house of talents which indicates whether a man is talented for some things that he can make money from. The best thing would be if each man lived from his gifts and talents doing a job he loved. It would probably bring considerable financial gains or wealth. So, for example, the Sun in the second house (if not badly positioned or in stressful aspects) can talk about large financial inflows and the ability to earn money. The Sun could talk about management, leadership, lecturing, stage and dance floor. Mars in the second house would talk about expenses (a person is talented to squander money, great attention is focused on acquisition, money can be the subject of struggles and problems, the Natus may lose money or there is the ease in spending money, money is gained through hard work...), and Venus talks of cash profits or assistance (also it may indicate that the Natus will have luck through sponsors, the acquisition from ornaments, perfumes, fashion, art, or in the case of affliction it can talk about prostitution, splintering, unnecessary expenses, over-indulgence...)

the Moon (changeable financial condition, agricultural jobs, botany, history, trade, food and beverages, working with household items), while the planet Uranus could bring the unusual twists and unexpected financial gains (physics, cybernetics, energy, electronics, computers, lottery...). One should have in mind that the whole horoscope has to be considered and then we can judge whether a person was born to make money. It can often happen that the Natus with the well positioned Saturn in the second house earns much more money than a person who has Jupiter and Venus there and in stressful aspects.

> *A friendship is better than kinship. You get relatives, brothers and sisters by some karmic pattern and you have no idea why this is so. We often think that we should love someone because he is our uncle, our brother or a nephew. Some tired and leisured man invented that*
>
> *"Blood is thicker than water", and following that rule we would have to put up with anyone who is our relative or has floppy ears after our grandfather.*
>
> Leo Daniel (Daniel Sijakovic)

**The third house** of the horoscope is about our environment, our neighbors, relatives, siblings, short journeys, transport, learning, intentions, decisions and everything that a man can learn by the thoughtful process. Heavy planets in the third house or the ruler of the third house in bad aspects or bad positions may indicate that the Natus has no brothers or sisters; he had lost his relatives, whether that loss is linked to illness and death or it comes from the interruptions of contacts. Heavy planets in the third house (Mars, Saturn, Pluto, Uranus and Neptune) can indicate the scientific intellect, deep thinking, mathematical mind, but it is mostly about people who suffer from depression, who are in quarrelsome mood, with pessimistic thoughts, severe mental illnesses or it can indicate speech defects and problems. The planet Mars in the third house can point to a quick and sharp intellect, a sharp tongue and mind, but it can also indicate a brother who is dominant or violent, or that the Natus has a problem with the relatives and close people. Many good planets in the third house are about artistic talents, creativity and skills to present themselves in the best light. The third house is associated with the traffic, therefore the cognition about our destiny in traffic or in traveling. The third house is about the means of transport, a car, the elementary school, as well as the intellectual force. For example, whether someone feels comfortable studying or not, whether the Natus is having difficulties thinking or develops a lightweight communication. Such conclusions cannot be deduced only from the third house, from the positions of the planets in it, but also from the position of the ruler of the third house (the planet that rules the sign), as well as the position of Mercury. The third house is often emphasized in travelers, traders, managers and agents. In case of a simple horoscope we can expect that a person will experience success in trade, and in case of an educated person, we can assume that he/she will experience the rise in intellectual activities, writing, courses and lecturing. Everything related to roads, communications and contacts is related to the third house of the horoscope.

> *Both rich and the poor cry equally, it's just that their tears do not hurt the same. A single man laments about when he will find a wife or a girlfriend, and a woman asks when her husband will stop drinking. A student wants easy exams and as much money as he could get, and the old people wish for good health and a few years more of life. We all want something, but mostly when it's not the time. A strange sort a man is, and impossible to satisfy.*
>
> *Leo Daniel (Daniel Sijakovic)*

**The fourth field** of the horoscope is the most personal and probably the most sensitive house, because it represents the embryo itself of the Natus, his family, his roots, genetics and his entire legacy. It describes the ancestors who died long ago, what kind of family he comes from; it talks about *the legacy* the ancestors left behind, father, mother or the older ancestors. The fourth field describes the home, the homeland, the character, the fireplace, the deep personal feelings and personal injuries. It talks about the end of life or the grave, about private business, in male horoscope it describes mother, and in female father. Since the fourth house is particularly sensitive, the astrologers forget that it should be treated as malignant. In essence, it is very dangerous, because it speaks about the manner of death and the grave site. As this is the water house, it possesses the occult traits and the special energy that is often not revived and awakened. For this reason, it should be treated as malignant, keeping in mind that its malignancy is far weaker than that of the sixth, the eighth and the twelfth house. If the malefic planets (Mars, Saturn, Uranus, Neptune, and Pluto) get there, the person comes from a highly stressed family, suggesting that there were warriors in the family, conflicts, confrontations and hatred, talks about the struggles of ancestors, so the Natus's life is not light and easy in this life, or he treats others thus. It can also talk about the loss of a home (somebody had died in the house, or that happened in the distant past), it can speak of family misfortunes, or that a person had been adopted (if there is a connection with the twelve series). Lots of bad planets in the fourth house indicate the unhappy childhood, poor living conditions while growing up, anxiety at home, sick parents or their disagreement. The Natus himself is not comfortable in his body and his skin, so he/she can grow to be a severe, closed and introverted person. More good planets in the fourth house indicate happiness and the gain through family, good kinship relations, peaceful and happy childhood, a beautiful end of life, admiration and popularity towards the end of life and the gain of a house or a family inheritance. Of course, the position of the Moon, the planets in Cancer, as well as the connection with Saturn and the eighth house have an important role. I am writing all this to prevent someone from banalizing astrology, and amounting assumptions and conclusions on the basis of only one good or bad planet in the fourth field. Astrology is an art that requires skill of understanding and connecting things. People who are withdrawn, sensitive and need to step back, while the fourth house is inhabited with the good planets, (by position and aspects) may find all the love, happiness and contentment in the family or in their own home. If there are more planets in the fourth house (whether in good or inharmonious aspects), a person can become a channel for spiritual forces, and often clairvoyant.

> *Make sure that you always do something in life and do not miss opportunities, because many of them will not be repeated. A favorable opportunity arises several times, and sometimes you have the opportunity to go to America only once, sometimes you meet the right woman or man only once. Maybe the person next to you is the right one, maybe it is the ideal partner, maybe it is someone who will love you for the rest of your life, and you act just like that, not taking things seriously, and then it happens that the nice people go away. Many times you have heard how a girl or a woman loved someone, but ended up in a marriage with a third man. Do not let nice people go away. You will regret it once. Do not let those who love you suffer. Just consider whether the person next to you is the one that you want to spend your life with. I tell you, do not waste time. There's so much you can learn about life and love, if only you are honest enough with yourself.*
>
> Leo Daniel (Daniel Sijakovic)

**The fifth house** of the horoscope is probably the happiest and warmest field of the horoscope. It is analogue to the sign of Leo and the testimony of energy, vitality, increased happiness and creativity. The fifth field signifies fun, high school, energy, love, sexuality, joy, play, hobbies, sports competitions, holidays, raffle and children. It indicates every form of creativity, satisfaction and fulfillment of desires. It is a house of energy and vitality. A good fifth house can point to a good and stable health. Many planets in the fifth house can give you success in sports, acting, love and games of chance. If the Moon finds itself there, it can signify a love that will be crowned by marriage, as well as the excessive love or devotion to the child. The Sun, Venus and Mercury in good aspects in the fifth house can talk about the numerous love affairs, physical pleasures and joys, many descendants and happiness that comes through children. People who were born to give and receive lots of love have the emphasized fifth field with the good planets. Severe planets like Saturn give few children, a cold and distant relationship with the children, obligation and problems with the children, as well as sexual problems, long and hard relationships, celibacy and long breaks between the two partners. Of course, a good position of Saturn in the fifth field may slightly fix the mentioned. Uranus, Neptune and Pluto in the fifth house can indicate the eccentric partners, difficult relationships, sexual perversions (not necessary or obligatory), the loss of children, difficulties with them, miscarriage, relationships with dangerous people, criminals, violent types, unemployed people... Mars may indicate the intensive sexual contacts starting from an early age, abortion, caesarean section delivery and the partners who correspond to the symbolism of Mars (impulsive, young, athletes, drivers...). It can also point to the hyperactive and energetic children, stormy relationships, frequent conflicts... The benefics with the good aspects give abundance and growth in the symbolism of all that comprises the fifth field, and the malefics in heavy positions and aspects speak about the disappointment, challenges, infertility, rape or the threats coming from sexual partners. It was noticed that the winners of large cash premiums in games of chance have the emphasized fifth field, regardless whether benefics or malefics were there, in good positions and aspects (this is also supported by the certain degrees of the Zodiac, the eleventh and the twelfth house). The natal horoscope should never be looked at superficially, or talk to the client about the miscarriage on the basis of Uranus in the fifth house, because the concrete and appropriate conclusions cannot be drawn only from the position of the planet. It is important to understand that the divine plan is made of many events and different experiences (some occurred in the past, and some are yet to be manifested in life through different symbolism). The astrologer must know the natal astrology and adhere to the Code of Ethics, which prohibits hurting the client. For this reason, one should be cautious in forecasts or any advice.

*Start the day with a glass of plain tap water. Stretch your body and get out for a walk. Say good morning to the neighbors with whom you haven't been talking for years. Water the withered flowers and empty the ashtrays. Do not let your apartment or room look like a garbage container. Try to laugh, even if you do not have beautiful teeth.*

*Nurture healthy and positive thoughts, because only then your body will be healthy, too.*

Leo Daniel (Daniel Sijakovic)

**The sixth field** of the horoscope is interpreted differently, and the traditionalists observe the ninth house of the horoscope as the house of illnesses, while the modern astrologers went a step further and attributed it to the features related to health, clothing, food, comfort, routine, everyday life, household, domestic animals, servants, people subordinate to us and completely committed, and all those who are doing something for us, as for a certain group of relatives (aunts, uncles...). The sixth field is the field of illnesses, but it has a very active part in the sphere of work, selection of profession, as well as the space and the way a person performs his/her job. Many good planets in the sixth field can indicate the responsible and good service, as well as certain happiness in the routines of life, while the malefic planets in stressful aspects speak about the delicate health and illness, so this house is active in people who take care about someone (doctors, pharmacists, therapists, healers, dietitians, homeopaths, people working with abandoned and handicapped children, special education teachers) and deal with social issues. The sixth field tremendously affects the mood and daily happiness, and a lot of planets indicate people with variable temperament and mood, prone to crashes and strong emotional reactions. The truth is that good and malefic planets in the sixth house reduce vitality and speak about problems, depending on which house the planet rules. For example, if the ruler of the eighth house is in the sixth house, a person may experience problems with the probate or inheritance. The succession will be reduced or completely omitted. If the ruler of the seventh house is in the sixth house, the husband may be in poor health, a charlatan or a crook, and in a better connotation a person can work with his/her spouse or partner. He/she can also be diligent, hard-working, responsible, or employed in some civil service (army, police, and administration, serving others...). A marriage can be sentenced to a disease or a problem, the Natus is a potential widow or widower. Such conclusions are made because the sixth house is extremely unfortunate and as much as the planets are well placed in it, they feel much better in other houses of the horoscope. Here's an example, Venus in the sixth house in good aspects may indicate that the person enjoys the beautiful work environment, works with women... If he/she was a doctor, he/she could be an endocrinologist. Venus could give the love for the pets, while, say, Mars in the sixth house could give inflammation, fever, chronic and acute diseases, everyday problems, a wild and aggressive house pet, and Saturn could give a hypochondriac or a workaholics, a job in the civil service or indigestion. In this way, we can generally look at the position of the planet in a particular house. I emphasize that the position of Mercury in the sixth house, or any other planet, does not have to speak about good or bad things, until the entire horoscope is not taken into account.

*As soon as the couple or lovers become bored*
*in a relationship there appears a "soul carer"*
*who is, most often, sleeping with your*
*girlfriend or a husband.*
Leo Daniel (Daniel Sijakovic)

**The seventh field** of the horoscope is extremely important, because it describes our complete opposite, everything that we strive for and that we want to become. It is the part of our being which will never be fully developed and awakened, but an everlasting part of the unconscious that has stunted in us, or has not been expressed enough. For example, if a person with the Ascendant (sub-sign) in Libra, gets Aries (as an opposite sign) in the seventh house, which should represent the energy that the Natus does not possess. In this case it would be a lack of confidence, directness and willingness (even though we all claim that we are full of confidence and irresistibly brave), the need for the person who would lead the Natus, the need for a dominant partner... In any case, courage and initiative are lacking. The seventh house of the horoscope is even more important, because it represents the other part of us that attracts us irresistibly; so the ascendant Aquarius is irresistibly attracted to Leo, but it is also in antagonism to him (Aquarius doesn't like chains and control and a partner forces her to his dominance, which leads to a deeper problem). In addition to the fact that it represents our partners, a spouse, our sexuality and friends, the seventh house often speaks about the responsibilities that a man acquires or never acquires through a joint relationship with someone. Regardless of whether it is about the conventional or unconventional partnerships, the seventh house is always about the people with whom we are in any way related to (a bond may not necessarily be an emotional bond). In addition, it speaks about the conflict, war, public enemies, antagonists, opponents, litigations... Many planets in the seventh house indicate intensive events in public or marriage, multiple marriages, or the various stages a man passes while being in a relationship with someone. In some cases it can speak of lawyers, politicians, actors and all those who have the need to present themselves in public. A good ruler of the seventh field, as well as the planet in strong dignity in the seventh field, points to good and stable marriage, the success through some kind of relationship or a happy union. Malefic planets in the seventh house indicate an injury in marriage, creating a strong hostility, fractures, hate, angry opponents and dissatisfaction coming through the partnership. So, the Sun in the seventh field gives the dominant partner, delayed entry into marriage, as well as recognition through marriage, while Mercury points to the marriage with an intellectual, writer, cousin; partners can be reached through contacts or correspondence, since future partner lives in another town (with the emphasized intelligence, or retarded in afflictions, upright and honest or deceitful and perverted in afflictions), or he had more than one marriage. Each planet in a particular house is one story that will largely depend on its good or bad position, as well as the aspects made with other planets. If, say, the planet Saturn finds itself in the seventh house in good dignity and aspects, it can often speak about the marriage of convenience, a senior partner, the cold and sustained relationships, celibacy and dissatisfaction. No matter how well-placed Saturn in the seventh house may be, it will never bring happiness, satisfaction, nice, light and airy marriage. In this case, happiness consists of the fact that marriage would be extremely long and lasting - "until death do them part". Jupiter can indicate affairs, multiple marriages, illegal marriage (in the affliction), and an educated partner, a foreigner, moral or immoral (poorly laid Jupiter in Capricorn and Gemini), it says that the Natus can experience happiness, prosperity and well-being by entering into marriage; he can leave the country or experience the spiritual progress through the partner. Anyway, the afflicted Jupiter in the seventh house is better than perfectly placed Saturn in the same place. The reason for such an argument is that in the first case we have enjoyment that can be hindered by all sorts of side issues, and in the second case we have a heavy stone that we carry, usually forever. Venus in the seventh field can give you a handsome partner, a dandy, or someone who likes to spend time in pleasant company (read - affairs). It can often happen that a partner is a musician or lives comfortably at the expense of others (do not be angry if Venus is there, and a partner does not play guitar or is not good-looking). Mars in the house of marriage sometimes brings heavy skirmishes, conflicts (and in some cases even violence), as well as a passionate relationship full of turmoil and tension. Uranus is rarely good in the house of marriage. It often brings unrest, divorce, and in severe cases widowhood and illness of the partner. If there are codes in synastry for the long, common life, Uranus will always bring the unexpected twists that are generally not pleasant. Neptune can rarely bring any happiness in marriage and sad are those who are trying to seek through the Neptune and find a sailor, a spiritual teacher and a man softly playing the violin in a partner. Neptune always brings bitter and harsh disappointment, a marriage with a dishonest and strange person, suffering and life difficult to achieve in practice. Often with this position of Neptune, we have a situation that a partner turns to drinking and all sorts of vices. Pluto in the seventh field can sometimes talk about deep, possessive and overly intensive relationships (pathological relations, fatal passions, strong attraction and desire for control and domination), as well as injury through threats, repression and control. Regardless of all this, it would be better if malefics were not found in the seventh house.

> *While we are healthy it is easy to give advice to those*
> *who are sick, prying into other people's business,*
> *playing smartly that it is pleasure to listen to us.*
> *It all takes awhile until misery knocks on the door;*
> *any wisdom of this world does not turn out good then.*
>
> Leo Daniel (Daniel Sijakovic)

**The eighth field** of the horoscope is probably the most intricate field and it certainly has not been explored too well until now. (More on this topic can be found in my work "The eighth house of horoscope - reward or punishment"). The astrologers know that the eighth field represents death and manner of death, illness, hazards and disasters (strong hostility, strange situations and different sufferings). Traditional astrologers entirely believed that the eighth house spoke of death and that it was not specifically related to other areas of life, but in addition to these we can talk about inheritance, the enemies who are hidden or concealed in some way, wounds, operations, fears, sexuality and occult powers. People with the strong eighth house often undergo the intense experiences which are not necessarily manifested externally. This field should be considered as a house of money that is not earned by work and it needs to be given the credit if someone became powerful or rich (without any trouble). The businessmen, doctors, military leaders, surgeons, mentally unstable persons, politicians and power brokers have the emphasized eighth field. This magical field has been insufficiently examined so far for the simple reason that a man does not know the secret of death, so the eighth house is extremely attractive, but in fact there is a huge ignorance about it. The eighth house of horoscope is considered to be extremely unhappy, and any planet that is found there is considerably weakened. Thus, for example, Saturn in the eighth field can provide a long life in a kind of isolation (especially if we have the ascendant Capricorn or Aquarius), an illness in old age, poor circulation or pain in the spine. Mars could bring the increased risk (although some argue that it is akin to the eighth house), scars, emotional wounds, occult powers, widowhood, struggle over inheritance, a strong erotic attraction and a strong libido. In women's horoscope it can talk about the unusual sexual partners, passionate people, soldiers, surgeons or doctors. This position of Mars simply drags the Natus into a problem, and we often see that, although weaker, he enters dangerous and risky situations. Venus and the Sun are not particularly lucky in the eighth house, especially if we are talking about the fate of the husband, father or some emotional relationship. On the other hand, the well-positioned Venus in the eighth field brings easy money and inheritance, but can rarely reduce love suffering. This is especially true if Venus is the ruler of the fifth or the seventh house. The position of the Moon in this field can seriously impair mental health and cause fears and phobias which can accompany the Natus in different life cycles. Also, the life of the mother should be considered (mother is of gentle health, emotionally unsettled, too tough or repressive, breakages followed her in her youth...), or mother financially helps the Natus and provides him with money. It would be good if such a delicate planet was not found in the house of death. The transcendent planets in the eighth house are useful if the Natus deals with the serious research, medicine (taking care of the old, the sick, the abandoned people and all those who have serious problems), in heavy industry, construction, mining or jobs that require a lot of energy and effort. Frequently, the emphasized eighth house of horoscope may bring a great wealth to the Natus. On the other hand, the psychological crises are inevitable and the only question is when they will be manifested. Everything that falls into the eighth field is quite weakened and distorted.

*You'll definitely be surprised that you do not succeed in anything, everybody else love, live, rejoice and earn, and you can only look at what is happening and cannot pull yourself together by no means. There are moments in which a man does not understand why he is so poor and unlucky, and nothing he plants blooms. You just need to accept that everything works perfectly, and that even your misery has deeper meaning. Of course, you will not understand. You should stay home; forget that you had big plans, and that you wanted to do something. If you go out on the street, you will not be interesting to anyone, nor will anyone be especially surprised to see you. People will not have much doubt if you're a movie star or an ordinary citizen who applied for the loan in some bank. Since everyone is a king in his own home, you should sometimes spend your life on your sofa. If you are employed and you work, then be happy to have a job. Always be thankful for what you get out of life, whatever that may be.*

Leo Daniel (Daniel Sijakovic)

**The ninth field** of the horoscope can certainly be called the God's house. It can bring the clear and deep insight to a man, clairvoyance, divine wisdom, distant exotic travels, philosophical mind, prophetic dreams and visions (clair-voyance, religion, spirituality and universal wisdom). The ninth field tells about our grandchildren, about the meaning of life, and points to the purpose and the man's existence. If there are planets in it, they can bring luck to the Natus during studies, abroad, or on some distant journeys. Also, it represents publishing, publication, serious, big commercials. It points to the development of a man from the apprentice to the master himself, a guru, a teacher or a spiritual leader. Weakly positioned planets in the ninth field point to the lack of support; and they also point that a person experiences suffering through learning, maturing and distant travels. The education is thwarted and the possibility to live abroad. A well-positioned ruler of the ninth house indicates that the person is the Heaven's darling.

> *Respect your bosses, authorities and superiors. You have to respect people who have achieved a lot more than you in order to "become somebody" one day. Do not just slander and gossip, because it is very ugly. If you want to become a great teacher one day, then you must be the best student and often a faithful servant. You will never be allowed to be great if you deal with small things.*
>
> *Leo Daniel (Daniel Sijakovic)*

**The tenth field** of the horoscope represents the very pinnacle of life and the maximum affirmation for one human lifespan. For someone the zenith of life is family, private business, the birth of a child, public speaking, book publishing... Everyone has the right to set himself a goal and the summit of existence. The tenth house shows what we strive for and whether we will become "somebody and something" in a lifetime. The tenth house is extremely important because it allows the Natus to replace or compensate for the disadvantages which he/she received at birth, or was conditioned due to other external factors. The tenth house allows a man to "correct" his destiny in a way that he becomes a "significant" person, or figure, by beginning to be independent from other collective events. How can we explain this? Imagine a man who was born in a poor, working-class family, in a small town, in bad conditions (bad or damaged fourth house of the horoscope). Let us imagine that the same person lived a hard life (poor diet, sad childhood, skimpy clothing, and bad relationship with friends...) and that the person in time, through some combination of life circumstances, managed to graduate from medicine. Immediately, the person strongly activates the tenth house, and this time receives the title of a doctor, which is the title and the tenth house in the horoscope. With this title, the person reduces poverty, others forget that he comes from a poor and small family, and also forget the Natus' unhappy childhood. Therefore, if someone is a doctor, or something significant, he is given the opportunity to meet different people and a chance to be upheld or respected. The same applies to a person who becomes a writer, a famous athlete or the best baker in town. In any case, the tenth house speaks of the rise, success, career, father, superiors and all those above us. If the tenth house of the horoscope is well-aspected and inhabited with healthy beneficent planets, a person experiences success in his profession regardless of whether it comes through ambition or reward. Lots of good planets in the tenth field give success beyond the capability, the ease, correction of poverty, as well as creating a certain image and a social prestige. If a person has a malefic in the tenth field of the horoscope (Mars, Saturn, Uranus, Neptune, Pluto) we can expect the family discord, difficult and agonizing death of a father or a cold relationship with the father, slow and difficult progression, strenuous working conditions and hazards toward the rise. For example, if the Natus has the Sun in the tenth house and in a weak sign (Libra) forming square with Saturn from the twelfth house, he can expect success until the certain part of life (through public performance), and then the fall caused by the powerful enemies, or the Natus himself by his bad moves. A well-positioned Saturn in the tenth field would point to the slow and laborious progress, which would be particularly manifested in mature years and stability carried by Saturn. We can as well talk about the politics or state honors. Mercury in the tenth house is about a writer, a traveler; Jupiter is about the judiciary, big business, and the Moon and the Sun about the public work. The tenth field allows the Natus to be relatively immune to the external events (collective events), to progress slowly and enjoy a greater degree of freedom. Each of us wants to become something and each of us welcomes his moment. Someone welcomes his zenith in the twentieth and someone in the sixtieth year of life. But of course, success is observed differently in America and in the Balkans. In wealthy countries the Natus could live his whole life and feed the family from one good book or a song, while in the poor countries talents will be of little value unless a particularly lucky star shines on them. Then the Natus rises above the crowd and experiences a slight success. The satirical novel "The Dead Sea" written by Radoje Domanovic speaks about the character of the peoples of the Balkans. We should learn from the great and wise people.

*If you progress in life and you become greater and greater, it is natural to become even more modest, because great people are really inconspicuous and quiet.*

Leo Daniel (Daniel Sijakovic)

**The eleventh field of the** horoscope is especially related to friendship and each kind of friendship. It symbolizes organizations, social institutions, political parties, alliances, easy connections, hopes, wishes and plans, sympathy, often even significant friendships and social affairs, pensions. The eleventh field carries happiness in itself, because it contributes to the fulfillment of desires and the realization of plans. This extremely beneficent field allows the Natus to be loved, favored, inspired, less burdened and often socially popular. The authorities also claim that this field is analogous to the sign of Aquarius, so it is linked to every kind of "brotherhoods" or formed alliances. Good planets in harmonious aspects in the eleventh field give auspicious opportunities, abundance, great life chances, providing a helping hand, patronage and light adventures. The malefics in the eleventh field supposedly give the loss out of each type of association and the disappointment through friends and all those who are close to us.

> *Some ancient peoples used to say that those who have no enemies have difficult fate. These old, wise men knew that the man does not feel good if there is no one to torment him. Life with no enemies, whether public or secret, is unthinkable today.*
>
> Leo Daniel (Daniel Sijakovic)

**The twelfth house** of the horoscope belongs to the group of the unfortunate (together with the sixth and the eighth field) and it is hard to estimate which house is more dangerous. The twelfth house symbolizes what has been before us, before our birth in the material body. The twelfth house reminds or falsely cheers the Natus to think of how he used to be strong once and participated in varios events that were not necessarily pleasant and comfortable. This house drains the Natus's energy and vitality, by pushing him into excessive action (notice that the people with the emphasized eleventh field are quite restless, ostentatious and ambitious). And, they do not hesitate to hurt you whenever they want or think is appropriate. Still, they are sensitive to sounds, insults, impressions, strong and pungent odors, surrounding events (for this reason, we often hear that they are sensitive, but that does not mean that they are effeminate or infinitely gentle and pleasant). If the twelfth field is damaged by the position of the ruler or the planets in it, it brings a sad and miserable life, unhappy and miserable childhood, lack of promotion and terribly powerful and annoying enemies. Like the eighth, the twelfth house also speaks about our fears and phobias, our secrets, hidden things, about the illness that will devastate and destroy the body, and the formidable forces that the formal science or medicine do not want to recognize and acknowledge. It speaks about the ghosts that possess the body, about the mistakes that we keep repeating daily, weakness and inability to change some life situation. In any case, the energy of this house forces a person to live far away from his/her family, confined, or in some kind of a cell or a cage, and it is often accentuated in paramedics, nurses, jailers, mental patients, secret agents, freemasons, people who retreat - monks, distant travelers, loners and those who enjoy atypical sexual preferences, missing people, orphans and all those unaware of their roots and origin. It symbolizes hospitals, insane asylums, prisons, and monasteries, remote and isolated places that are not easily accessible and visible. It indicates every kind of loss, danger out of darkness, a mad animal's bite, the death under unusual and difficult circumstances, shark's bite, getting lost in the jungle or some other remote spot. On the other hand, it is noticed that people with good positions of the planets in the twelfth house can expect help from the guardian angel, as well as significant financial losses. However, regardless of these mitigating circumstances, it should be understood that all that was found in the twelfth house tends to be difficult to express or never to be expressed in a sound and comprehensive manner. Thus, for example, the Sun in the twelfth field can speak about the lack of the father (the father is weak, careless, drinks, doesn't care about the Natus or doesn't even take interest, or in the second case he can be of gentle health or the Natus has no realistic image of him) or about the husband's illness, as well as of work in the laboratory and hospital facility. In the best connotation it can give a secret love affair with a married man who will sooner or later hurt the person, and a father who is a special and spiritual man (which is less likely) and the emphasized ambition (the reader must not think that the ambitious ones are only those with the Sun in the tenth house). All good variants and options of the positions of the planets in the twelfth field are very rare and special, so if we have Saturn there (no matter that the traditionalists say that Saturn loves to be found in the twelfth house), it brings seclusion, grave mistakes, strong hostilities, the attack on a person even if it is not his/her fault, the threat from the darkness, serious and insidious diseases which can take years (if the ruler of the horoscope is also bad). We often see injuries and abandonment of dear people, and the unhappy force that drags a man to the very bottom or into some problem. The power of the planets in the eighth and in the twelfth house is best treated by active work (we are talking about difficult and hard work), spiritual exercises, stretching, prayers and meditation (which in practice are not proven to be the most effective because I experienced the biggest problems exactly with people who constantly cleanse, pray, fast and work on self-realization). The Natus with the emphasized twelfth house is more often wrong, he is his own enemy, and gets into trouble that can be avoided. As I have already mentioned this is the house of celibacy and a solitary field, it is often emphasized in spiritual leaders, teachers and gurus. Today their learning is observed with great enthusiasm, but the real truth is that the spiritual teachers are not able to live the mundane life because of the many planets in decline, expulsion, in the sixth, eighth or the twelfth field. Then they choose the monastic life, accept celibacy and close to themselves, which is much better than to live opposite to their own energy. If people enter into the spiral of the twelfth field consciously and peacefully, they may slightly improve their mood and alleviate accidents, but can never fully neutralize its effect, nor make a place like this a living paradise. If the planets in the twelfth field have a healthy dispositor or their effect is mitigated by good aspects and powerful dignity, the Natus manages to find a proper and adequate solution for the years of crises, or find a way to be relatively happy and satisfied. The real truth is that these people have been hurt many times and they often hurt the others.

# THE SECOND PART

# PLANETS
# THE SYMBOLISM OF PLANETS

Astrology is a celestial alphabet, quite complicated and coded, and therefore, one necessarily has to be particularly skilful and wise in order to read and interpret it. Astrology is also the skill of making words and sentences, which appear by combining astrological symbols. These astrological symbols are defined with three factors: planets, signs and houses. With the combination of these three factors we get the ability to create images, which present potential events. One should have in mind that linking up of symbols is a dynamic process, and one should understand that one position of a planet in a certain astrological house or sign may signify 1000 things, but we are not completely sure whether the natus (the born) will live only one part of the story or each of the 1000 things. For example, if there is a possibility that the natus hurts his spine or back seriously, and that has not happened to him, it does not mean that it will not possibly happen one day although the natus has never had problems with it. So, there is time when the potential event could happen, which falls into the domain of predictive astrology. However, even if there is an indicator of spine injury, that injury does not have to be in real time, but something else will happen in the same astro-symbolism (for example, father's hard life, slow progress, heart problems...).

Astrological symbol always signifies more than one thing; it is a dense field of information, which contains more possibilities in itself. In other words, there are innumerable images and situations, which the natus (the born) will live, which possibly exist in him and which he could possibly develop, if he chooses certain life paths. By combining one symbol with certain other symbols we get a range of words and sentences, which emerge in certain situations. Firstly, it is important to realize the basic meaning of each symbol through three basic factors – planets, signs, houses. In each astrological card, each symbol describes the person, ourselves, what lives in us, our inner characteristics (subjective level), but also things around us – objected, manifested, outer level (what happens in reality, in the material world), which is expressed in the sphere of concrete people and concrete events. Planets are active carriers of destiny, whereas signs and houses are the background. Planets are the concentrate of events, the focus and essence of one horoscope. In the astrological sense, all lights that we can see in the sky are called planets and therefore, it is said that there are ten planets, although in reality that number is not correct – the Moon is the earth satellite, and Pluto has been classified into dwarf planets recently. However, that is not important for astrologers, but only for astronomers. Personal planets are those which are nearest to us (in astronomical sense planets which are nearest to the Earth). The Sun and the Moon belong to that group, and in astrological sense they are called Lights as well – Luminaries (lights are extremely important), then Mercury, Venus and Mars. As they are closer to the Sun (in astronomical sense) these planets move faster, and therefore, they are more significant for a personal destiny, whereas distant planets are slower and their influence is more shown at the mundane level (at the level of world events). Personal planets are significators (astrological expression which means indicator) of everyday life.

## Astrological signs

Signs are the other part of astrological alphabet (there are 12 of them). In contrast to planets, astrological signs are static and they usually color the picture of the entire horoscope. Each planet has a sign which it rules, manages, and therefore, there is a great similarity between the planet and "its" sign, and difference lies in the fact that the planet is active, and it presents a dense sign – the concentrate of the sign. Twelve signs make the circle of 360 degrees, and each of them has 30 degrees, while the planet can only be on one degree, and it is concentrated there – there it has the strongest influence and from that place it receives all the information (quivers and vibrations) from the cosmos. Astrological signs are, therefore, far more diluted than the planet and a lot weaker as far as direct influence is concerned. Signs present a psychological background, genetics (ancestors), which speaks through us and we behave as marionettes. How can we understand that? Well, for example, if there were violent people, warriors and so in our genetics, then it can be seen through the position of Mars in the sign of Taurus in the square with Pluto. This automatically means that somebody of our ancestors wishes us to be sharp, rough and violent. To which extent we will be that, depends on our consciousness and our spiritual development. We can also inherit artistic qualities from our ancestors. They can, for example, be reflected in the tight conjunction of Mercury and Venus. We can automatically inherit the talent for writing or singing, but to which extent the same talents will be expressed depends on the rest of the horoscope, where the natus lives, what his family is like, and whether he has the wish to develop his talents. If we observe one of the greatest musicians and composers of all times, Johann Sebastian Bach, we find that he comes from a particularly musical family – uncles were musicians, father was a famous musician, and analogously to that, it is natural that somebody who comes from such a family is musically talented. If his ancestors had been warriors by chance, Bach may equally have been talented, but there are small chances that his life would make it possible for him to get education, to be engaged in music, and live from music. He must have lived some other parts of the story and aspects, which had been left by his ancestors to be possibly corrected and improved. In any case, talent is carried through genetics, as well as personal traits, the color of eyes, hair, height etc.

Astrological signs describe the planet by pointing to what is inside, distant past, what it is made of, what was there long time ago, what the ancestors were engaged in, which fields they knew best, where they stayed most, what they were the best and dominant at, where they made mistakes most and repeated certain life lessons...). For example, if there is the planet Mars in the sign of Libra, it would mean that potential emotional conflicts, partner problems, which date back to the past, are hidden in Venus (which rules this sign). Zodiac signs should never be mixed up with constellations, because they do not correspond to the real constellations in the sky, although they have the same names as constellations. Therefore, if the planet Mars is on the 11th degree of Cancer, it does not mean that the same planet is in the constellation of Cancer. It is, actually, in the constellation of Gemini, but it will be discussed in more detail later.

Each sign is described by planets, which rule it. Each sign is ruled by the certain planet (some signs by two planets):
Aries – Mars

Taurus – Venus

Cancer – Moon

Lion – Sun

Virgo – Mercury

Libra – Venus

Scorpio – Mars (Pluto also feels well in this sign; Scorpio is akin to it)

Sagittarius – Jupiter

Capricorn – Saturn

Aquarius – Saturn (Uranus feels well in this sign; Aquarius is akin to it)

Pisces – Jupiter (Neptune feels well in this sign; Pisces are akin to it).

Astrological signs, twelve of them, can be classified into certain groups according to:

# Elements, quality and gender

**Element** – basic nature of a person – temperament

Astrological signs in relation to the element are classified into: *fire, earth, air and water signs* – and each of them psychologically corresponds to certain temperament. For example, a person who has an emphasized water element (a lot of planets in water signs) is, according to the temperament, *phlegmatic*, a person who has the emphasized Earth is primarily *melancholic*, Air – *sanguine*, and fire – choleric. According to the emphasized element, people can be classified into four basic psychological types. Choleric is, regarding behavior, fast, hasty, explosive, impulsive, extrovert... Melancholic carries some melancholy and sadness in himself, he is slow and turns toward past (retrospection). Sanguine person is very adaptable, tough and resistant in various situations. Phlegmatic is very calm, retiring in a certain way (as well as melancholic); he can be prone to depression in a bad setting, while the choleric and sanguine people, basically, do not carry that characteristic and are primarily connected with liveliness and agility.

# The classification of the signs of Zodiac according to gender

According to this classification signs are divided into *male* (fire and air) and *female* (earth and water), while in the Zodiac circle they are arranged and connected so that male signs always go first, and then female (Aries – Taurus, Gemini – Cancer, Lion – Virgo, etc.).

**Quality** – the basic style and way of reacting to circumstances. The classification according to quality is very useful in natal, as well as horary astrology. According to quality, Zodiac signs are classified into: **cardinal, fixed and mutable.**

*Cardinal signs* (Aries, Cancer, Libra, Capricorn), which point to the beginning of seasons or the beginning of something (in any area) – the beginning of spring is defined by the entrance of the Sun into the sign of Aries and then we say that Aries sign begins, the whole new Zodiac year begins, as well as Zodiac cycle and new energy. Cardinal signs are related to beginnings, initiative, impulsiveness, for everything new and for leadership. The role of cardinal signs is to enable beginning and instigation.

*Fixed signs* (Taurus, Lion, Scorpio, Aquarius) are responsible for stability and permanence of everything which exists in them (either planets or houses). In contrast to cardinal signs, which are hasty but of short breath, fixed signs are slow but permanent. It can be positive, but also really bad. The role of fixed signs is to enable stability and permanence. Also, fixed signs do not have the ability to free themselves from something easily, if that thing is not good or does not function. For example, a person can be at the working place, which he or she does not like, or stay in a marriage which does not please them. However, a good thing is that fixed signs can pursue their aims long and chronically, and if the aim is noble and good – then they persevere until the end and they often triumph. Here the accent is on the idea that a man should be brave for a long time, to persevere longer, to dream longer and aspire to something (under the condition that the choice is favorable).

*Mutable signs (Gemini, Virgo, Sagittarius, Pisces)* are signs which are between cardinal and fixed, according to their quality. They are the least stable – but their role is not to be stable but to provide changes and communication between differences, thus making life easier, more bearable and simpler. There are things which are extremely difficult and stiff in this world. The role of mutable signs is to make things simpler and enable agreement and change from one life topic to the other without stress, struggle and conflicts. The role of mutable signs is to unite and enable changes, but they point to certain instability, which can be mirrored in all spheres of life (partnership, money, health, friendship etc.)

Each astrological sign has its specific code, which contains its element and quality: 4 elements X 3 qualities = 12 signs.

# Zodiac Houses – life areas

Astrological houses are the most personal thing in one horoscope, because they appear from the moment of birth, from the moment of first breath, when a child comes out of mother's womb and the cry resounds through the delivery room that a new soul is incarnated in the physical body and material world. They are what we get last – the last formed in the cycle of designating one new destiny, one new life story. The very degree of the Ascendant (or rising sign) is the beginning of incarnation. That is the moment when the Creator says – Now!

That would mean: *Old soul, formed in a new body, play the role, which I assigned to you, love, be happy, fight, learn how to protect yourself. Play the best you can on the life journey, develop skills, help yourself and people, give your best, meet yourself, people, the world and accept with gratitude everything you have and you don't have – your skin color, race, your parents and all the rest which I offered to you.*

There are 12 astrological houses exactly and they respond to each sign of Zodiac. A planet presents and describes a person (an actor) and replies to the question who it is all about; the sign gives a psychological description of the planet – it describes what it is like or what it is made of – that is presented by a planet and replies to the question what something is like (of what kind, material, intensity...). Astrological houses describe the place and the potential space, where something will take place. If the natal Sun is in the 6$^{th}$ house, it points to the possibility of accomplishing aims, the self and the career, by treating and curing diseases or it shows that father is ill in a way, he endures, suffers or it points that the natus wins his enemies and diseases. However, the Sun will in this case be accomplished by "serving" somebody or something, which is the 6$^{th}$ house of the horoscope. Astrological houses describe the place or the area of life, where something will happen. They are more personal and therefore, more important than the sign. Planets are expressed through the house and the sign, in which they are.

## *Classification of houses according to quality*

They are divided into angular, succedent and cadent houses.

Angular – 1, 4, 7, and 10th house (Ascendant, IC, Descendent and MC). These houses are also called the Angles of horoscope. Everything that exists in the angles is always expressed more and it is much stronger. Thus, the planet is always more active, more striking and expressed if it is in the houses 1, 4, 7, and 10. However, it does not mean that it is positioned the best and that it is the happiest. Everything that is in angular houses wishes to be expressed at any price – therefore, there is no chance that a planet would not act if it found itself in angular houses. These houses (1, 4, 7, and 10) are called the antennas of horoscope because they absorb everything and then emit it back. The more planets in angular houses, the stronger and more conspicuous the horoscope is, but that does not mean that it is better and more special by any means. Thus, if you do not have planets in angular houses, it does not mean that you are not with good qualities or special.

Succedent – 2, 5, 8 and 11th house. These houses are akin to fixed signs. What exists in these houses, in contrast to angular, is expressed more slowly and a lot of time is necessary. It is necessary to invest more effort in order to express it. Take this also with slight caution.

Falling (cadent) – 3, 6, 9 and 12th house. These houses are akin to mutable signs and point to instability and things, which are subject to changes. During the estimation whether it is better to have something in succedent, cadent or angular house one should be cautious, because sometimes it is good to have something precisely in cadent, and sometimes in angular house. For example, if Mars is found in the 10th field, and the planet Saturn in the 7th field, such arrangement automatically means that both parents will suffer, that the family will suffer, that there are certain doubts regarding the future marriage and partner etc. (this is only a simplified demonstration).

However, the position of Mars in the sixth house can significantly be harmful for health and mental frame of mind, but also it can conquer and eliminate all the enemies. On the other hand, the position of well-positioned Sun in the 11th field, influences a lot better financial circumstances than the position of the Sun in the 6th house of horoscope (under the condition that the Sun governs money). Thus, nobody has a perfect horoscope and some part of life, unfortunately, always has to suffer.

## The classification of astrological houses according to element

They are classified into: fire, earth, air and water houses.

*Fire houses* – 1, 5, 9 (akin to Aries, Lion and Sagittarius).

These are the houses of life, vitality, light, play and creation and therefore, they are the most important for maintaining life, vitality.

*Earth houses* – 2, 6, 10 (akin to Taurus, Virgo, Capricorn).

These are the houses of value, related to concrete material and strict destruction of man into material (spiritual identity is lost and one strives for accumulation of wealth, material growth and rise).

*Air houses* – 3, 7, 11 (akin to Gemini, Libra, Aquarius).

These are not personal houses, but the houses of relationships because they always speak of relationships with other people (brothers and sisters, neighbors, partner, friends, company). Therefore, the light is cast on others, on people who surround us, who work with us, live with us, sexual and business partners.

*Water houses* – 4, 8, 12 (akin to Cancer, Scorpio, Pisces).

These are supposedly the houses of emotions, feelings, intuition, talents and occult powers. In any case, a lot of positive and negative feelings are in the game and a strong feeling for what surrounds us or what happens to us, is always present. Thus, you cannot stay aside and just observe, you have to take part emotionally.

**Significator** is mainly the planet, which rules the sign, which naturally belongs to a certain house. For example, Mars is the ruler of Aries, which naturally presents the 1st house, and therefore, Mars is the signifier of everything, which the first house presents. Venus could, according to this, be the signifier of everything presented by the 2nd and 7th house (food, diet, earning, marriage, partner, public...).

**The ruler of the house** is the planet which governs the sign, in which a certain house begins, and therefore, it is more important than the significator because it is more personal.

## *Intercepted (enclosed) signs and planets*

For those, who do not know what the intercepted (enclosed) sign or planet is, I will mention that in the system of uneven houses it happens that some houses are bigger (bigger than 30 degrees), so it often happens that in some way they swallow the sign. For example, the peak of the 4th house begins with the sign of Aquarius, and ends with the sign of Aries. Here, the sign of Pisces, which is insufficiently incarnated, is swallowed, enclosed, hidden or suppressed. If it happened that in the same case Venus was in the sign of Pisces, we could certainly say in astrological language that this planet is intercepted or enclosed. Intercepted signs are equally important, but one should not forget that the strength or weakness of a certain event or life topic is expressed through the planet, so it is the main and the most active carrier of destiny. Thus, it is a lot more striking when the planet or a few of them are in the enclosed sign, than when signs are enclosed, and their rulers freely arranged (they do not endure the position of intercepting).

The meaning of the intercepted sign:

It points to things that happened some time ago. Everything which is included in it is expressed later in life. If it is in the present, it is always hidden and secret; it presents all which is not seen enough at the moment – lost (misplaced) things, secret relationships, those which do not turn into marriage. For example, if there is an intercepted sign in the 1ˢᵗ house (and thus in the 7ᵗʰ), the person, whose horoscope it is about, will express one part of personality hard, probably later in life, and there is possibility that something regarding partner relationships is secret.

Some rules regarding **intercepted** (enclosed) planets (are the result of experience and research lasting for many years, and huge, astrological database):

The intercepted planet should never be identified with the retrograde planet.

– the planet even in the best cases and positions creates troubles for the owner of the horoscope.

– the planet usually speaks of hard work, renunciation, the loss of light, difficult circumstances, delays, and with its activities it strives for complications and in a way becomes seemingly less visible.

– the planet is often good for research, scientific work, devoted work, medicine, criminology, psychology and medium abilities.

– the planet is, from the practical point of view, always weaker than the planet, which is in the enclosed sign, but its demonstration is always deeper and more significant than other planets.

The intercepted planet should always be observed with the ruler of the ascendant, planets in the angle or MC.

The intercepted planet always draws attention with its position, so although it is expressed later in life, the owner of the horoscope feels its effect everyday and it lasts *only Forever.*

The intercepted planet will always suffer in its position, no matter in which period of life it gets active. In other words, it will not be completely healthy and strong.

One should pay attention especially to whether the ruler of the ascendant is presented by the intercepted planet.

The intercepted ruler of the ascendant does not necessarily mean weakness, disease or death, as it is stated by some authors.

The intercepted ruler of the ascendant can point to superhuman quality, better results than *normal position*, but everything will, in a way, often be masked and somehow stay less noticeable.

The intercepted planet brings a lot of suffering if the dispositor is bad, and the rest of the horoscope stressful.

The intercepted planet in some cases can speak of weak health, psychological difficulties, widowhood, or some other kind of suffering, only if there are more indicators for such a thing and in situations when the lights are weak together with the ruler of the ascendant.

The intercepted planet is in some cases good for spiritual work, but there are no rules which confirm this.

While analyzing the quality and meaning of the intercepted planet one should necessarily take into consideration the sign and position in the house, where the planet is. The same position clearly points to what it is about, so the astrologer just has to especially pay attention to it.

The intercepted planet should not be identified with Yod configuration, although with its position the universe tries to point to certain problem, karmic debt or life mission.

The intercepted planet can be especially useful in karmic astrology because it automatically points to the load which the natus carries from the past. With the position itself, the intercepted planet helps the karmic astrologer to create clearer and more precise images regarding some other lives.

The intercepted planet often does not bring peace to the owner of the horoscope and it should be treated with special attention because in some parts of life it could cause serious problems, spiritual or physical suffering.

Demonstration of the intercepted planet is never direct, but it can be presented by concentric circles and spiral movements.

The intercepted Venus in horoscope is often the sign of certain love suffering, which of course, does not have to last forever. For a more concrete picture, it is necessary to study its dispositor, as well as other factors in the horoscope.

The intercepted Mars in horoscope is critical towards himself and others, so at some moments in life he does not show enough courage, bravery and driving wish; the same goes for libido, where we do not treat libido only as sexual energy, but life wish and impulse for creating and creative work. However, in some situations it has been shown that the intercepted Mars gives a workaholic and demonstrates crazy courage, which is frequently identified with the situation of *block out* (this is especially the case if Uranus is tightly connected with Mars). Regarding the fact that these situations are not that frequent, one should hold to the first setting, which speaks of the intercepted Mars.

The intercepted Mars was shown to be very malefic, no matter whether it was found in favorable or unfavorable houses of horoscope. Greater attention should always be given to personal planets, than to distant, transcendental planets, which are in the enclosed sign.

The intercepted planet often speaks of behavior in the previous life, as well as future events which are created, changed or fixed by the natus, depending on the understanding of some problem.

The intercepted planet should be observed as a karmic debt and its position is never accidental.

The intercepted planet usually needs a lot more fuel or energy, and therefore, it suffers and endures in some normal conditions and circumstances, which do not demand special attention and engagement.

The intercepted planet is able to come to some hidden and deep life truths, which are often around us, but others do not have opportunity to feel or detect them.

The intercepted planet in some cases helps in occult knowledge, astrology and healing practice.

The intercepted Mercury often contributes to nerve overstrain and oversensitivity, especially if it is found in the sign of Virgo, Scorpio and Pisces, as well as in unfavorable houses of horoscope.

The intercepted Mercury is not necessarily the sign of a problematic child, car theft, the loss of keys or similar things in its symbolic, nor does it speak of the loss of memory and weaker intelligence.

In some cases the intercepted Mercury brought speech defects, which were noticed in its retrograde moving or when it was found in the sign of Capricorn or Pisces.

The intercepted planets in the 5th field often pointed to infertility, and in some cases sexual harassment or abuse.

The intercepted Moon spoke more frequently of infertility than it showed itself in a favorable light.

If the Sun is intercepted, then we can speak of a special father or husband, and it does not necessarily speak of widowhood or problems in marriage.

The intercepted Venus showed itself as more dangerous if we speak about love pleasure, suffering in marriage or emotional relationship than other planets. In some cases it spoke of partner's weak health and numerous other problems. Here the astrologer has to check the other factors of the horoscope, in order not to hurry with fatalistic prognosis.

If the astrologer notices that some planets are positioned uncomfortably, and that they are in the enclosed sign, it is obligatory that the astrologer draws client's attention to the problem and starts with the treatment of them, which in a certain way suffer and endure in their position.

The intercepted planet speaks more frequently of deeply hidden secrets, than the owner of the horoscope is aware of or ready to admit.

The intercepted planet should never be mixed with singleton planet.

The intercepted planet should not be treated as the planet of unused energy; we could rather say that the energy is used incorrectly, and in some cases its strength is spent more than it is desirable or necessary.

Intercepted planets can demonstrate only exceptional results or can be only problematic (malefic). Even when they show exquisite quality, hard work, suffering and self-denial are behind.

# Unaspected planet

Unaspected planet deserves special attention and a really voluminous book could be written regarding this topic. However, we do not have space for such a thing, so we will try to present this astrological topic as simply as possible.

When a planet is unaspected, then one should pay attention to it. It is important to understand that none of the planets should be alone. Thus, it would be great if the planet would create some aspect towards other planets. If the planet creates none of Ptolemaic aspects (conjunction, trine, sextile, opposition, square), then we say that it is unaspected – it is in a way left to itself. Even if it is well-positioned (in the sign and in the house) sooner or later the time will come when some problem will emerge. Unaspected planet is not a malefic planet, but it particularly endures, and therefore, astrological houses, in which it rules, as well as planets in governing houses suffer with it. If it is greatly positioned in the sign and it is in the strong house, then it will give a lot to natus with certain limits. Here, I will give one example: Natus (rw) had in her horoscope Venus on the 8th degree of the Libra sign and in this case it ruled the ascendant (the first house) and the same Venus was unaspected. The woman was really special, intelligent, capable, talented, cheerful and optimistic, exceptionally successful, but she had one disability – she stayed short and barely reached the height of 140 cm. Here we should have in mind that the planet rules the ascendant (physical body, appearance, character, health, temperament...). As far as her emotional life is considered (Venus is the signifier of marriage and love life), the following is the case – this wonderful person stayed widow early, and the next partner was blind and a lot older than her. This is only one example of the unaspected planet. Not all examples are so drastic, but if I used my astrological database, you would see how this is not the best arrangement in one horoscope. Also, there are examples where the unaspected planet did not cause huge damage, but in their cases the rest of the horoscope was extremely strong.

The beginner is not advised to make fatalistic estimates according to what he has read – there have to be at least 3 astrological indicators, which point to the same thing.

## The lonely (isolated) planet – Singleton

The very expression lonely planet means that it stands somewhere isolated and alone in relation to other planets, which are separated from it by the horizon or axis IC-MC. Some authorities believe that singleton planet acts differently in certain life stages – it can be super active or completely inactive. If it is about personal planets, the effect is more present and distinct. The accent should not be given to transcendental planets, but one should take into consideration when Jupiter and Saturn are concerned. In any case, accent is on certain passivity of a planet, which could one day draw attention on itself. It should be estimated which house is ruled by the singleton planet, so if it is marriage, it can point to the period of celibacy, stillness, and loneliness, in order to become more active in social sense in some part of life. One client had a singleton planet in her chart and it ruled partnership. She had been shy and reserved, in order to become completely promiscuous around the age of 25. She lived completely unrestrainedly a few years (she often changed sexual partners), in order to get married suddenly, she settled down and gave birth to two children. Today she lives in a peaceful marriage, she is completely dedicated to raising her children and it could be said that she is a caring mother. That would be one example of a singleton planet. It is important that astrology practitioner estimates what it is about and which areas of life the lonely planet corresponds to. Also, I encourage the astrology practitioners to research this topic better, because, unfortunately, there are not many quality texts about it, which could help to understand it better.

# Rising sign – ascendant

Through the rising sign (ascendant) we could approximately conclude what the natus's purpose is, or to approximately assume what experiences he will go through, how he will feel like and what he has to learn (which life lessons). Of course, this is only the simplified idea of the rising sign (ascendant). Each astrology practitioner has to know that the ascendant is the most important thing of each horoscope and that 70% of all answers are placed in it, answers which are necessary in order that a man understands himself a little better, and in the end people who surround him (family, partner etc.) Each degree of the ascendant (the circle contains 360 degrees) carries its mythological story or some other story, which can be approximately discovered by knowing the degrees of Zodiac, as well as Sabian symbols. The sign which is opposite to the rising sign (ascendant) is its essential opposite. Authorities assume that it is something which the natus is missing, something that he will never understand, accept or achieve, so if on the ascendant is the sign of Aries, the authorities assume that he will never understand what is opposite him (Libra), presented through refined relationships, excessive tenderness, kindness etc. Thus, somebody, who has Aries on the ascendant, should practice all types of relations, to learn something about the needs of other people etc. Taurus is missing what Scorpio has, and Gemini what is contained in the sign of Sagittarius etc.

## Aspects in Astrology

The aspect presents the angular relation between two planets. The aspect means the view. If the planets look at each other from the natal horoscope they oblige to some relationship, interaction and event – if the event takes place in the natus himself (on emotional, psychological or quantum-physical level), or if it takes place in completely real life. If a person gets some serious disease, it means that in his base (natal horoscope), there is a good potential for something like that to happen. Even if nothing stressful happened in reality, the same man experienced a lot of struggles, many crises, different sufferings on the emotional and psychological level through his planetary aspects, just we, as observers, are not allowed to peek into his inner being – we see only a man and make conclusions based on what the eye sees. However, emotional and psychological levels also create events and real situations. It means what we are like in our hearts, in our minds – such things happen to us. Planetary aspects can be stressful (disharmonic) and favorable (harmonic). The terms "positive" and "negative" aspects are today considerably abused, because astrologers do not often have opportunity to understand in which way some planet influences the other planet. It is not because astrologers do not have enough knowledge, but because it is about a lot more complex scheming – it is about innumerable relations, which create the whole one world, which is at one moment very complex and stressful and at the other moment very favorable and efficient. Some aspects are generally favorable, and some unfavorable and such a bad, unfavorable contact – aspect is called affliction, and the planet, which is in unfavorable aspect, is said to be afflicted. Even when the planet is unfavorably aspected, it can give a lot in the sphere of material and spiritual, but all these gains come through struggle, effort, conflicts, rises and falls, waiting, postponement, and what is most important, one always goes by a more difficult and roundabout way. I have seen people with extremely stressful horoscopes, who developed into wonderful characters and very harmonious horoscopes, behind which weak characters were hidden. Thus, the astrology practitioner will have a lot of problems while analyzing one chart, and in the end it turns out that he had made a serious mistake when estimating some destiny, psychological profile or when using prognosis. My advice is not to divide people and aspects into "good" or "bad" because what we think to be "good" or "bad" is often based on individual experience or our "blurred" perspective of that thing.

# Main (Ptolemaic) aspects

Aspect is an angular relationship between two planets – two planets seize certain mutual angle and the number of degrees, which they seize, determines the type of aspect.

There are five main aspects, and these are: conjunction – 0°

Opposition – 180°

Trine – 120°

Sextile – 60°

Square – 90°

*Conjunction*

Conjunction represents two planets which are together. The most exact conjunction would be that those two planets are on the same degree and minute. However, there is allowed tolerance as far as the distance of planets in conjunction is concerned and that allowed tolerance is called orb. In the narrowest sense of the word, those planets are positioned in the same sign, and at the distance from 0 to 10 degrees, that is, the biggest orb, which is tolerated, is 10 degrees. In the Vedic astrology the allowed orb is a lot bigger – planets are in conjunction when they are found in the same house. For example, the planet Mars can be found on the 3rd degree of the constellation of Scorpio, and Venus on the 27th degree of the same constellation. Vedic astrologer thinks that they are in a conjunction and that they influence each other. In tropical astrology, something like that is not possible, so there is an allowed orb, which points to whether and to what degree planets influence each other.

As far as conjunction of two benefics is concerned, we can imagine that the Sun and Venus are between these two planets and such a conjunction has the nature of Sun and Venus. However, when two malefic planets are together (for example Mars and Pluto), then this conjunction is threatening; it presents the concentrate of two evils and it can mean fall, suppressed aggression, serious disease, hatred, violence, danger... (this is only the simplified idea of the aspect itself). Bad conjunction has the nature of malefic, and therefore, the conjunction of two malefics is the same as Saturn was between them. The very nature of conjunction is the most similar to Saturn because Saturn is the planet which naturally longs to bring something down to one point and disable it to develop in a physical sense (in spiritual sense it is not completely so). Therefore, the effect of Saturn is the strongest precisely in conjunction. Conjunction means the intensive relationship and we should estimate which conjunction is favorable and which is not. According to some authorities, conjunction is the strongest aspect, but it is the best that astrology practitioner spends some time studying the aspects.

When analyzing some aspect, one should, of course, take into consideration in which houses planets rule, beside their basic nature. Thus, we will always accept gladly that rulers of happy houses are in our conjunction (e.g. the ruler of the 1st house conjunction the ruler of the 9th house), while we will become worried if the ruler of the Ascendant is in conjunction with the ruler 6. (illness, enemies, losses...), 8. (dangers, death, diabolic powers...) or 12th house (prisons, mental and physical anguish, hospitals...), although one can live with that. If the conjunction is mixed (either it is the combination of benefic and malefic, or the ruler of a good house and malefic house) it is necessary to observe how those planets feel in the sign where they are, as well as the rest of the horoscope.

A planet is in *cazimi* if it is in conjunction with the Sun in orb, within the distance smaller or equal to only 17' – 17 arc minutes. It is very rare and very favorable. For everything, which that planet represents, there is somebody or something very powerful, which favors its growth. Whoever is represented by this planet, it seems as if he has the great protection of mighty powers. However, there are astrologers who believe that no conjunction with the Sun can be happy, even if it is Cazimi conjunction. Actually, the planet is **combust** if it is found close to the Sun. However, the planet's burning differs in strength and intensity. If Saturn is closely burnt by the Sun (for example in orb smaller than 5 degrees), that is deemed to be exceptionally unfavorable conjunction and combustion. There are astrologers who think that Mercury is not hindered by the Sun's combustion (close conjunction), whereas, for example, it disturbs Venus a lot. When a planet is combust, it, according to some astrologers, does not have any strength, but it is quite damaged. According to some, it is the same as when a person gets serious burns, and he is susceptible to atmospheric influences and all other things. However, I have encountered burnt planets, which could give particularly favorable results. The astrology student has to spend some time studying the effect of combustion (close conjunction with Sun). Thus, the planet is combust if it is found in the conjunction from 1 to 12 degrees with the Sun. If the conjunction is exact with the Sun (until 17 minutes) then this conjunction is called Cazimi conjunction.

## *Opposition*

Opposition shows two planets, which are positioned one opposite the other and they build the aspect of 180 degrees. Planets can be in opposition even if they are not in opposite signs, while some astrologers believe that planets are in opposition only when they are found in opposite signs (Aries – Libra, Cancer – Capricorn etc.).

The permitted exception from 180 degrees is maximum 8 degrees. Generally speaking, opposition is considered to be among negative aspects. However, in the Vedic astrology, the situation is not such. For example, Mars and Moon can make opposition and it is considered to be a happy setting (one of the codes for wealth and physical strength). In tropical (western) astrology, such a thing is inconceivable and prohibited. Planets which look at each other through opposition cannot find a mutual language easily. Planets strive to separate themselves sooner or later, although the starting attraction can be strong, because it is about oppositions that attract each other. But, it is difficult to live endlessly in opposition and striving to break and end the bond. This is not often true for Saturn's opposition. If

Saturn watches something from the aspect of opposition, it strives to keep that thing, no matter whether the owner of the horoscope likes it or not. The basic nature of opposition is similar to Uranus, as if Uranus was between the planets, which are in opposition. It means that sometimes it acts suddenly, hastily, unpredictably, capriciously, with a lot of stress. Each opposition at deeper (karmic) level presents the thing, which was started a long time ago, but due to the loss of knowledge, persistence or means it stayed incomplete.

## *Trine*

Trine is a very beautiful aspect. Planets which create the angle of 120 degrees have a great quantity of mutual understanding. The permitted orb is 8° (some astrologers allow bigger orb). Trine seems as if Jupiter and Venus are between the given planets (great benefics, happiness, abundance). It describes events, which are favorable, which unfold with easiness and have a good perspective. Disregarding the fact whether the planets are connected by trine, during analysis we try to get the best out of the symbolism of other planets. However, if Saturn creates trine towards some other planet, it will certainly be good and useful, but with a dose of "bitterness". Here, we can certainly take bitter – melancholic relationship with very good results through time. For example, trine of Saturn and Sun can create the need to build career and business patiently, and therefore, the character is formed really favorably with numerous limits at all levels. The results are and can be great, but with a very difficult background.

## *Sextile*

Sextile is also a favorable aspect, however, authorities believe that it has weaker effect than trine, but this should be taken with reservation because I haven't found proofs that sextile is "of smaller range" and less strong than trine. We can imagine that between the given planets there are

Mercury and Venus, which connect them, thus emphasizing their nature of harmonious communication and intelligence. Signs which look each other through sextile are those which are combined well, and those are air-fire and water-earth. On the other hand, cooperation (sextile) is promised by the signs male-male and female-female. The permitted orb is somewhat smaller: from 0 to 6 degrees (some astrologers include orb until 8 degrees).

## *Square*

Square does not promise anything good or easy. Some astrologers go that far and believe that nothing good can be born of the square aspect. On the contrary, when the planets are in the mutual square, there is intolerance, great dose of aggressiveness, tension, the need to use great energy, which is usually very rough. There is no stillness with this aspect, and the prevailing relationship among them is of "Mars" nature. Also, it regards something which is rarely finished, which makes it similar to opposition. However, in contrast to opposition, which strives to separate participants, the square always brings them to conflicts...The permitted orb for square is 8 degrees. This aspect has the nature of Mars, so the planets in the square can be interpreted as if Mars was between them. The square is an aspect, which speaks of things that we started long time ago, in some past life and now we are facing some similar energy, but in accordance with time in which we live. It would be ideal if we lived each unfavorable and tense aspect with the least possible fury and stress. In other words, if we do not have something or we do not succeed in something, we should laugh more, understand and accept more what we do not understand, do not like or do not have. A positive side of the square aspect is that it constantly and tirelessly strives for a change, action, effort; it gives enormous unconscious and physical energy, it strives for ambition and real material achievement. Thus, the square, besides stress and conflict, can rarely give inertia. On the contrary, there is always a tendency to build something. If the natus in his natal chart has a lot of squared aspects, it is quite certain that his life will be full of changes and turbulences; natus will strive to be better, to solve something, change or fix, but it would never be completely easy. It would be ideal, if the natus had a multitude of good aspects besides squared aspects, as well as strong planetary settings, so that life wouldn't be only stress and suffering. Successful people always have squared aspects in their charts. They are strong motivational fuel and in the best case they have great results at school, sport or work. Of course, one should understand that the square between Mars and Venus is incomparably more difficult than the square between Jupiter and Mercury, even when Jupiter rules unfortunate houses (6, 8 and 12).

## Secondary (minor) aspects

It is necessary to hold to small orbs (1°–2°) in order to take into consideration some of the following aspects. These are: Quincunx – 150° Semi-Sextile – 30° Semi-Square – 45° Quintile – 72° Bi-Quintile – 144° Septile – 51° 3/7

Secondary aspects do not have strength as main aspects, but they can influence natus. They supposedly contribute to occult powers, talents and other qualities, which are not seen at first sight. Quincunx and Semi-Square are the most important of all minor aspects. They can also be very dangerous, if the rest of the horoscope is not quite fortunate, either. Semi-Sextile and Quintile are favorable and contribute to good luck and talents.

### Orb

Orb is the allowed tolerance from the expected number of degrees. It is expressed in degrees (and minutes). Aspect is said to be exact if it is close, that is, if its orb is small (to 1 degree). Aspect is completely exact when two planets are on the same degree and minute of corresponding signs. Two planets are in a partil aspect if they are in corresponding signs and if they are on the same degree (disregarding minutes). For example, Mercury on 9 degrees and 20 minutes of Gemini and Jupiter on 9 degrees 44 minutes of Aquarius. Close aspects are very personal and also important, more important than the aspects of wider orb. The most important and the most expressed are close aspects of personal planets.

### The lack of some aspects

If there is not even one opposition in the horoscope, then the person cannot get into open conflict, which is not always good. If there is the lack of square, then the natus does not have enough initiative, fuel, energy, wish, passion... It is clear that the lack of trine is not desirable because then everything goes painfully and with difficulty, and similar is with sextile. There are horoscopes with a lot of aspects, which describe a dynamic life with a lot of opportunities to do something. On the other hand, there are calmer lives, which are described by natal charts without many challenges, and without too many (challenging) aspects. It does not mean that it is better to have an exciting and dynamic life with a lot of challenges; I use this opportunity to mention that there are different lives and different destinies.

### Applying and separating aspects

In order to conclude whether the aspect is the aspect of applying or separating, one has to know the speed of planets' movement. Usually the planets are arranged according to the following order (from the fastest to the slowest): the Moon, Mercury, Venus, Sun, Mars, Jupiter, Saturn, Uranus, Neptune, and Pluto. However, sometimes that movement is not such: if some planet slows down before the beginning of the retrograde movement, or if it has started directly recently, but has not reached its average speed – that is, it is slower than its average speed. Applying aspect is that angular relation between the planets, which strive to reach the exact aspect. For example:

Mercury on the 22nd degree of Gemini and Mars on the 24th degree of Aquarius are in the applying trine because Mercury is faster planet, and therefore, it will arrive to the exact trine with Mars.

Applying aspects speak about future events because they speak of movements in advance and they become stronger in time. Generally, we will take that they have a bigger weight. Separating aspect is that angular relation, in which planets move away from the exact aspect. For example, Mars on the 27th degree of Pisces and Uranus on the 23rd degree of Virgo are in separating opposition because Mars is faster and goes away from the exact aspect with Uranus.

# Retrograde and direct planets

When the planets move counter-clockwise, then it is said that they move directly, and what we mean by that is "normal" or standard movement. If a planet moves "normally" or directly, then it has the most powerful strength, then it does its best, whatever it is and no matter how big it is (if, for example, Venus is direct, but very weak in its sign, it can give only as much as its true strength is, which is measured by its position). Vedic astrologers find that retrograde planets are very powerful, so their power and quality are expressed later, and also they have a habit of saying that retrograde planets have a lot greater spiritual potential. However, astrologers from the west do not agree with that – they think that a retrograde planet is always weaker, and therefore, it brings harm depending on its position, the strength of the horoscope and the condition of dispositors (their rulers). However, it happens occasionally that, looking from the Earth, it seems that the planets move backwards, which is not true in reality – they do not move really backwards, but it just seems like that, looking from the Earth. It happens due to the fact that the Earth itself turns around its axis and together with other planets around the Sun, and that movement of the Earth and the Sun leads to illusion that other planets move in the opposite direction from the normal movement. This phenomenon is called the retrograde movement of planets.

Each planet decreases its speed, with which it moves, before it starts its retrograde movement, slows down, stops and starts in a retrograde direction. Likewise, when it should start directly, it slows down, stops and starts directly, forward.

What are retrograde planets?

- Most frequently they point to the loss in the symbolism of that planet (if it rules marriage, it will more often point to a problem, than to some special and striking partner, although it may happen sometimes).

- Problems, repetition, return, retrospection, losses, doubts, delays, search, disorientation, secrets, knowledge, spiritual knowledge; they are very important in karmic astrology.

### Retrograde Mercury

It points to losses in the symbolism of Mercury – keys, wallet, car, hardship with children, studies and exams, mental susceptibility, illogical things, stubbornness, speech problems.

In a good setting, it can point to a particularly intelligent person, with developed consciousness, talented and wise. Here we speak of knowledge that can hardly be found on the Internet or in books.

Retrograde Mercury is favorable when it is necessary to return to something that we had started long time ago (job vacancy, work, writing a book, studying, restoration of something that was started a long time ago, and it was not fruitful in the past).

Mercury is retrograde three times a year, and it lasts 20 to 24 days.

### Retrograde Venus

If it is found in some horoscope, then one should especially pay attention and study its setting, as well as aspects.

It points to more than one marriage, love sufferings and troubles, affairs, sometimes to widowhood, disagreement, worries, enemies in marriage, the loss of money...

In a favorable setting, it may point to a really important partner, exceptional connection with some person, strong karmic bonds, love until death; partner can be a friend, Teacher, and Guardian Angel; the bond with some person is unbreakable (even if there is disagreement).

In the example of a woman, who was born on June 6th, 1980 in Belgrade, Serbia at 1:05 pm, Venus is retrograde in conjunction with MC and in conjunction with Mercury.

She entered into relationships with a lot of partners, but she has never been satisfied. On one occasion, she met a man, with whom she had lived in an illegitimate marriage for eight years. After that, he left her, however, their relation has never stopped existing – today they are great friends and her ex-partner helps her financially and with giving her advice. She says for her ex-partner that he is her Angel and that life with him was the most beautiful period of her life.

Retrograde planets can be observed in the following way:

If, for example, Venus rules the 4th house of some horoscope, and it is retrograde, it automatically points to some parents' weakness or to some family problem, which is constantly being repeated or which lasts long. The aspects and position of Venus speak more about the problem, but here we try to simplify things, in order that an astrology practitioner could understand the effect of retrograde action. In any case, take retrograde quality, firstly, as a potential problem or obstacle in life, which you will solve easily or which you will solve and understand only partially. All this should not be perceived in a fatalistic way and with anxiety. Retrograde planets have positive effects as well, which I have stated in the book.

If the transcendental planets are retrograde (Uranus, Neptune, Pluto), do not worry a lot about that, because their retrograde action lasts for months and there are generations of people, who were born with the same retrograde quality. However, if personal planets are retrograde to Saturn inclusive, then it is particularly important. The most striking retrograde action is connected with Venus.

Venus is retrograde every 1.5 year and it lasts 40 to 43 days.

## Retrograde Mars

Astrologers usually have a habit of believing how retrograde Mars is a coward, weak, sportsman, weak soldier, who is afraid and who worries, an impotent man... In reality, it is not exactly so. So, if retrograde Mars is positioned in your natal chart, it does not mean that you are not a good lover or that you are not capable of being a great sportsman.

Retrograde Mars influences life decisions (natus is insecure, although he/she has enough strength); it contributes to health problems (illness of head, bones, muscles) and love problems (here we speak about disagreement, and not about impotence, as some suggest); perfidious enemies; danger lurks where the natus least hopes; deep and not understandable hatred... (This is all valid in really hard settings, including the other weaknesses of some horoscope).

In a favorable setting, natus manages to overcome troubles and dangers, results are seen through hard work; success in any undertaking, struggle sometimes speaks of great wealth, heroism, honors...

Important note: One should never begin affairs, projects or anything else when Mercury, Venus and Mars are retrograde.

Mars is especially malefic when it is in transit towards the natal horoscope in a retrograde movement. Then, it is capable of making a lot of damage to the owner of horoscope.

Mars is retrograde every two years and it lasts 58 to 81 days.

Retrograde planets have a very important role in horary astrology because they point to the return or repetition of something (Will my husband come back to me? Will I find my wallet? etc.).

Example:

In this example, we observe the retrograde Mars, which builds a retrograde sextile with Pluto. The Stellium of planets is found in Aries. This is the horoscope of a military leader and general, who served in the Napoleon's army and he distinguished himself by incredible merits and courage. What is characteristic for this man is that he is the example of the first black general in the French army. One should have in mind that the natus was born in 1762. He was brave and fearless. Mars is on the very beginning of the sign of Scorpio (in its domicile) and it is retrograde. Here the astrology practitioner can see how the retrograde Mars is not a coward (in some texts we can find that the retrograde Mars is not brave). Lights (the Sun and the Moon) in the sign of Aries, as well as squares of Pluto towards the stellium in Aries, contribute to his courage. Therefore, there is a lot of fire, courage and bravery. Here, the retrograde Mars in Scorpio did its best – beside bravery, it contributed to the fact that the colored people could become famous and great army leaders. As this general lived in the 18th century, we could freely say that it was something new and unusual. Childhood of this general was also imbued with suffering – he was born as the son of a slave, who was bought by his father, and later sold to slavery again (the Moon conjunction Saturn in square with Pluto).

**Alexandre Dumas- Thomas**
NATAL CHART

March 25, 1762
11:29:44 AM
Local Mean Time
Jeremie, Haiti
18 N 39   74 W 07
Time Zone: 0 hours West
Tropical Placidus

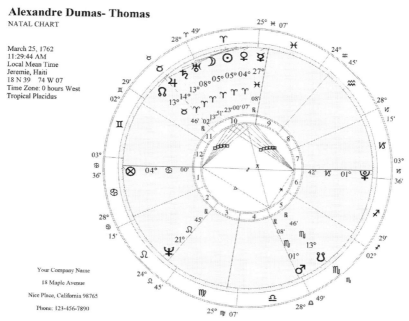

Here, Mercury is retrograde and on the degree of the exaltation of Venus (27th degree of Pisces). Mercury signifies children and younger generations – general's son lived in extreme poverty, in order to become one of the most famous writers of all times later in life. We speak of Alexander Dumas – Father, who wrote famous works "Count of Monte Cristo", "Three Musketeers", and many other. Here the retrograde Mercury, on the degree of the exaltation of Venus, gave something exceptional – son and grandson of this famous general are famous Alexander Dumas – Father and Son, giants and colossi of world literature, descendants of slaves and famous leaders.

The retrograde Jupiter symbolizes the interruptions of studies, problems in foreign countries, illegality, money losses, loss of honor and name, problems with male descendants, sometimes ill children, infertility…

In a favorable setting, it speaks about strong character, white magic, spiritual exaltations, religious leaders, life in a good family, welfare, pilgrimage, contact with foreigners (partner is a foreigner or a very important person), then house abroad…

The retrograde Saturn symbolizes other long and serious (chronic) diseases, disagreement with father, poor childhood, problems with bones and joints, tiredness, family worries and suffering, father's illness, slow advancement, weak hair and teeth, spiritual suffering…(only if other factors confirm that; when astrologers state something, they have to take part out of the whole. It means that there are a lot of people with the retrograde Saturn, who have healthy and strong hair, and good teeth. The same goes for all other settings – they are always taken out of the whole, and they should be observed in such a way).

In a favorable setting, it speaks of constant success, advancement, healthy and long-lived body, good life, and asceticism, of help, which arrives from powerful and prominent people, respect and a good reputation…

# Stationary planets

Stationary planets are those which are at a standstill (as if they were not moving, waiting to begin to move) – between direct and retrograde, or retrograde and direct movement, and therefore, there are two types of stationary quality: from direct into retrograde movement and from retrograde into direct movement. A planet is stationary if its speed is reduced to less than 10% of its average speed. Stationary planets can sometimes be extremely dangerous and malefic. Some authorities have a habit if saying that a stationary planet is, actually, benefic, but an astrology student had best deal with this topic in more detail.

# Planetary dignities

Planetary dignity describes how a planet feels in the sign, in which it is. Each planet has a sign, which it rules, and when it is set in that sign, it is in its domicile. It means that it is at home, the owner of that space, it completely controls that space, determines its contents and quality and rules that place (Lord). Also, there is the place, where the planet is exalted, where it feels well and we say that the planet is exhilarated. Some astrologers believe that exaltation is the strongest place, where a planet can be found, but it is not completely true because the exalted planet depends on its dispositor (the planet which rules the sign). If the dispositor is weak in the sign and aspects, the exalted planet will give good results during a great part of life, but over time it will certainly lose strength and quality, and therefore, contribute to poor results. Imagine that in some chart, marriage is represented by Venus in the sign of Pisces (exaltation), and its dispositor (Jupiter) is in the sign of Virgo, in the square with Mars and Saturn. The marriage would be great and of good quality, but certainly problems appear later, which is impossible to avoid. Thus, the planet in its domicile is always stronger than the exalted planet, because it is the ruler of its house on its own, and it does not depend on dispositor. The exalted planet expects a lot from itself, it is very "tense", gives good results, and due to that it is often the case that when such a "tension" relaxes, the natus feels broken and exhausted in some part of life. It is as if you want to be good, wonderful, and beautiful constantly, and that only good things happen to you... However, you meet people, who do not like you or do not understand you, you encounter numerous obstacles, physical and material, and you simply break or give up. The opposite place from the domicile is called exile or detriment, and the opposite place of exaltation is fall or dejection (casus). When a planet is in the sign of its exile (detriment), it feels very weak there; it draws strength out of the ground which won't do it good, it is fed with the food which does not make it strong, it cannot grow and develop its qualities to the maximum, it feels anxiety and hostility, which is manifested in a thousand ways. As far as the fall of a planet (casus) is concerned, the situation is similar, only that the planet has a tendency to experience the very bottom or fall sooner or later, and this fall can be observed metaphorically or literally – imagine one object made of glass, which fell from the chair one day and was broken to pieces – the same object was in that case completely useless, broken...The situation is the same with the falling planet. When we, for example, say that the planet Mars is falling (the sign of Cancer), we foolishly believe that the person does not have muscles, does not have strength, cannot experience erection and similar things, which is a complete nonsense – the person just cannot act in a stable and normal way all the time. That person cannot enjoy one life situation constantly, cannot stand still, cannot feel complete pleasure or joy, he/she needs something more... The person, who carries the falling planets in himself, does not know what he misses, what would make him happy, but feels that something is wrong. Then the same person sets off to search in order to satisfy what he/she longs for – if it is love, the person starts flirting, an affair, looks for new partners, new sexual experiences, new people... Sometimes in that search he/she can find peace and happiness, but somewhere hidden behind there is tendency that something goes wrong in the future... If it is about physical activity, the person goes in for strenuous sports, in which it is necessary to devote a lot of time to body (tennis, body building, martial arts) and in that way the "bad" Mars in fall is calmed down, its fury weakens because it is active, there is something to muffle it and make it calm.

Sometimes the manifestation of the falling planet is manifested through illness, emotional weakness, frustration, block-out, serious spiritual conditions, constant changes in the career or something else, fury, aggression, deep and not understandable hatred etc. So, if a planet is weak, it is always susceptible to transits, directions and progressions of other planets – it can go to extremes, it can make something extraordinary, and then fall and break completely... One will wonder: can a planet in exile or fall bring good results? My answer is: Yes!

A planet in exile or fall can make a man work on himself constantly, be better, change, progress, become the best in some field, but it is only in the domain of material gains and business success. Emotionally, falling planets give a lot of frustrations, which are especially seen when a man gets old, and he is not able to run after the tennis ball, to change jobs or women... Then, the natus comes to the situation that everything which he worried about, comes to the surface, only it is incomparably more difficult to fix the damage...

When can a falling or planet in exile give favorable results?

- When its dispositor is positioned very well (favorable house, strong aspects, favorable degree of the Zodiac...).
- When it is directed towards reaching material aim (studying, competing, money earnings...).
- When the rest of the horoscope is very strong (and especially the ruler of the ascendant and personal planets).
- When the natus is born in the good surroundings (good upbringing, good education, material welfare, nice parents...).

- When it is in the favorable house, and not damaged by malefic in any case, nor does it make conjunction with the ruler of the 6th, 8th and 12th house.
- When it is in the mutual reception with the other planet or just builds good aspects.
- When the north node and south node do not make unfavorable aspects toward the falling planet.

However, when a planet in fall or in exile signifies interpersonal relations, the way of thinking, marriage or things alike, than it cannot in any case give favorable results, no matter what the causes of that crisis are (e.g. some people, due to some problem, accuse parents, church, society, neighbors, professors and others, and they do not understand that certain sphere of their lives could not give good results, even if they attended the best courses of motivational speakers, or if they were good as angels themselves). In the folk language, if a planet is weak, then the house, which it rules, is weak, and it will last only forever.

Example:

**Robin Williams**
NATAL CHART

July 21, 1951
2:34:08 PM
Daylight Saving Time
Chicago, Illinois
41 N 51   87 W 39
Time Zone: 6 hours West
Tropical Placidus

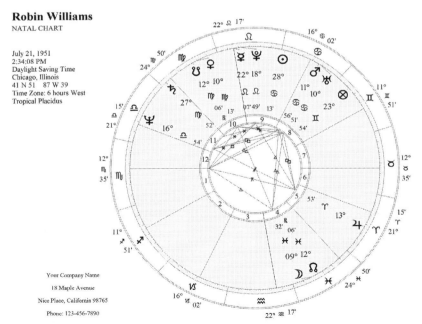

This is the horoscope of the famous actor, Robin Williams. Scorpio is on the Ascendant (water, female sign, introvert, and deep, magnetic, sensitive, unpredictable...). The ruler of the ascendant is Mars in the sign of its fall (Cancer) in a very tight conjunction with Uranus. This conjunction contributes to talents and strengthens creative powers, but does not influence well physical strength and psychological stability. So, Mars as the ruler of the ascendant is weak and tender, prone to influences and impressions, inclined to daydream, artistic, sensitive, and subject to everything, stressed... in other words, when it is so sensitive, then it is weak and susceptible to transits, weak solars and directions. Its position in the $8^{th}$ house additionally complicates things and decreases the strength of the character, contributes to sadness, falls and depression... Water signs are sensitive, receptive, easily influenced from aside...

Venus, which in this case rules marriage, partnership, all life pleasures, public, and scene is very weakly positioned (in the sign of its fall – Virgo) and is additionally damaged hard by the malefic conjunction with the south node. Venus, set in such a position, works well for material success, work, devotion to job, money gains, but it influences poorly life satisfaction, happiness, partner relationships... In brief, it makes the natus sad because beside work he cannot experience additional satisfaction. It should be mentioned that earth signs are melancholic, female, introvert, and it also applies to water signs. The Moon is also sensitive in Pisces (water sign), builds a tight conjunction with the north node, which also doubles his creative skills, but influences mind and psyche unfavorably. The Sun, as the most important factor in tropical astrology, is in Cancer (water again) on the degree of the falling of Mars, and we have already said that Mars is extremely weak. A lot of factors indicate weakness, and two planets are in the sign of their fall.

However, how do we see the actor? On MC Mercury in Leo is with Pluto – he is immensely funny, attractive, communicative, inexhaustible, he knows how to get the crowd on the feet, to inflame and cheer it up – in brief, perfect in public, at work, with other people. That's the way we see him. Mercury is an angular planet – it is on the very top of the horoscope, and therefore, it is at the same time the "antenna", which determined profession and what the natus would do. However, the same planet cannot substitute for happiness or love, since we have to find them in ourselves, and sometimes in others (parents, partner...).

The real truth is that the actor had a lot of problems, falls, suffered from depression, was addicted to alcohol, and had difficult love affairs which ended ingloriously... Apart from being very talented, successful, popular and dear to people, he did not find a way to help himself, he did not find enough light in himself, so his life was ended tragically in the period, when he could have created most and given his best.

In this example, we have seen that falling planets can inflict serious damage, if a man is tender and with artistic inclinations, and lives in a very fast and cruel world. Then, he reacts tumultuously to everything, which happens around him (in astrological sense, to transits and other movements of the planet, which are manifested in everyday life).

Furthermore, each planet has its specific degree of exaltation in the scope of the sign, in which it is exalted, as well as degree of its fall, where it is on the worst degree for himself.

The Sun is falling in the sign of Libra, and the very degree of its fall is the 19th degree of Libra. The Sun is in the domicile, when it is in the sign of Leo, and the 19th degree of the sign of Aries is the place of its exaltation. The Sun is really weak in the sign of Aquarius (the sign of its exile).

The Moon is exalted in the sign of Taurus and it is deemed to be very fruitful in that sign, and the very degree of exaltation (exhilaration) is the 3rd degree of the Taurus sign. The Moon rules the sign of Cancer (domicile), it is especially weak in Capricorn (exile) and Scorpio (3rd degree of Scorpio is the place of Moon's complete fall – there is no light).

Mercury is the ruler of two signs (Gemini and Virgo) and therefore, is in the domicile of both signs. It is supposedly exalted on the 13th degree of Virgo, and somewhere you can find that it is the 15th degree of Virgo. In Vedic astrology there is belief that Mercury primarily rules Virgo, and then Gemini, which should mean that it is stronger in Virgo. Take this also with reserve. Opposite the exaltation is the sign of its fall – Pisces – so Mercury in that sign is expressed really badly, especially on the 13th degree. Sagittarius is the sign, where Mercury is in exile. However, I have found many times that people with Mercury in the sign of Sagittarius are incredibly capable and intelligent. Of course, it does not depend only on the position of Mercury.

Venus is in the domicile in Taurus and Libra (some think that it is more dominant in Libra, and more prolific in Taurus), but it is exalted in Pisces on the 27th degree. It is supposedly the most fairy-tale place in Zodiac, where all the inspiration, imagination and rosy side of our reality come from (we have seen that father of famous writer Alexander Dumas has Mercury on the very place of the exaltation of Venus, and Mercury signifies children; also Hans Christian Andersen has Venus on the place of its exaltation – he wrote the most beautiful stories and fairy tales for children). The opposite of it is the 27th degree of Virgo, which is the place of the Venus's fall – and it points to all possible losses. Venus is in exile in Aries and Scorpio, so we say that Venus is extremely weak there, although it is most possibly a lot weaker in Aries than in Scorpio. Mars is in the domicile in Aries and Scorpio, and exalted in Capricorn on the 28th degree. Mars in Cancer is the weakest because it is influenced by emotions, fury and different impressions (here we do not speak of physical strength, but of tendency that something goes wrong in the symbolism of the house, which is ruled by Mars). The degree of fall is opposite of exaltation – 28th degree of Cancer – and this is the weakest place for Mars in Zodiac.

Jupiter is in the domicile in Sagittarius and Pisces (Vedic astrologers give priority to Sagittarius over Pisces), and it is exalted in the sign of Cancer on the 15th degree of

Cancer. Supposedly it is the place where love, mercy, compassion are in focus...

Jupiter in Capricorn is in the sign of its fall, and the exact degree of fall is the 15th degree of Capricorn. Supposedly, it is the place, in which a person completely falls into an ambitious delirium, dazzled by success, money and achievement.

Saturn is in its domicile in the signs of Capricorn and Aquarius, in exile in Cancer and Leo, and exalted in the sign of Libra. The exaltation of Saturn is on the 20th degree of Libra, and fall on the 20th degree of Aries, and the Sun is exalted on the 19th degree of Aries, and in fall on the 20th degree of Aries.

Uranus is in its domicile in Aquarius, in exile in Leo, exalted in Scorpio on the 11th degree, and in fall on the 11th degree of Taurus.

Neptune is in its domicile in Pisces, in exile in Virgo, exalted in Aquarius, and in fall in Leo. The degree of its exaltation is the 21st degree of Aquarius.

Pluto is in its domicile and exalted in the same sign – Scorpio. The degree of its exaltation, the 3rd degree of Scorpio, is the degree of Moon's fall, and degree of its fall (3rd degree of Taurus) is the degree of Moon's exaltation.

How do we come to the fact that some planet is in its domicile, exaltation, fall or exile?

Well, astrologers believe that if a planet is in the sign of its domicile – opposite it is the sign of its exile and if it is in the sign of its exaltation, opposite it is the sign of its complete fall and ruin. Of course, this is a really simple explanation. Astrologers came to the conclusion when a planet is strong and when it is weak, according to the observations, which have lasted for thousands years.

**Peregrine planet** – it is the planet which does not have some basic or main dignities – it is not well positioned, nor is it in the sign of its weakening, like the Sun in the sign of Pisces, Mars in the sign of Virgo, Venus in the sign of Cancer, etc. Supposedly such a planet is not interesting, it is left to itself, it does not attract attention, and it gives average results even when it tries hard to achieve something. Some astrologers believe that there's no hope for such a planet, so they call it homeless, wanderer... Supposedly, misfortunes follow it beside good aspects and the best will. One should be careful with such a statement. Astrology practitioners should analyze this topic more.

**Triplicity** – is also classified into the favorable dignity of a planet. Supposedly it is regarded as really favorable, but not so good in order to make wonders and do its best. So, this planet feels comfortably, pleasantly, it can partially distinguish itself and develop to some point... Thus, it supposedly cannot reach that far...

As far as fire planets are concerned, they should be in the sign of Aries, Leo and Sagittarius. Example: the Sun in the sign of Sagittarius or Mars in Leo.

As far as earth planets are concerned, it is necessary that they are found in the sign of Taurus, Virgo and Capricorn. Then we say that they are in triplicity. Example: Mercury in the sign of Capricorn and similar.

As far as air planets are concerned, they should be found in the sign of Gemini, Libra or Aquarius. Then, we also say that they are in triplicity.

As far as water planets are concerned, they should be found in the sign of Cancer, Scorpio and Pisces. Then, we also say that they are in triplicity. Example: the Moon in the sign of Pisces.

## When is the planet alone in the house or when does it happen that there is not even one planet in the house?

When there is only one planet in the house, then it is not a special problem. One should check in what essential dignity the same planet is, what aspects it builds, and what the case with its dispositor is (the planet which rules the sign, in which it was found, if it is not in its domicile). So, if there is only one planet in a certain house that does not mean in any case that the house is lonely and not emphasized.

If there are no planets in some astrological house, it does not mean that the house or field of life will not be accomplished. Each house has its ruler and it determines how intense the strength of that house is.

### Is a planet in the house stronger or the ruler of that house?

There has been debate among astrologers about whether the ruler of the house is stronger or planets, which are found in the certain house. Here the astrology practitioner is encouraged to study and research this topic in more detail. In my personal opinion, advantage should always be given to the ruler of the house over the planet, which is found in the house. Here is the example number 1.

The Sun is in Virgo in the 7th house in good aspects. The ruler of the 7th house is Mercury in Pisces. The Sun (although a benefic) rules the 6th house of the horoscope (enemies, diseases...). Do you think that some marriage will be good even without hard challenges? Even if the Sun rules a healthy house, Mercury in fall (the ruler of the 7th field) will make a huge damage. I think I have answered the question whether advantage should be given to the ruler of the certain house over the planet which is found in the house. Certainly, the planet, which is found in the house, carries its energy, increases and diminishes it, brings in quality, but advantage should never be given over its ruler.

Example number 2.

The peak of the field begins with the sign of Aries. The exalted Sun is in the 7th house, and the ruler of the 7th field is Mars in Cancer (fall). What do you think - can this marriage survive without great crashes and stress? In my data base, I have dozens of examples, where only benefics inhabited the house of marriage, but the ruler of the marriage was always weak. All marriages ended, unfortunately, with divorce, they were accompanied by serious problems and ex-partners have never stayed friends.

Example number 3.

The peak of the field begins with the sign of Libra. Jupiter, Mercury and Mars are in a tight conjunction in the 7th field. Planets in the 7th field do not endure any damages from aside. The ruler of the 7th field is Venus in Virgo (fall) in the 6th field afflicted by Uranus and Saturn. What do you think – are benefics in the 7th field able to preserve this marriage? Of course, they are not. So, never give advantage to some planet in a certain house over the ruler of the house. If you do not believe this, feel free to check.

## A Stellium

Some astrologers believe that more planets in one house give special strength and strengthen the house. It can only partially be true. A stellium means that 4 or more planets are in the same house or sign. The allowed orb is 10 degrees, and sometimes 12 degrees between the planets in the Stellium. There is a belief that planets influence each other strongly in the Stellium depending on which houses they rule, and whether they are benefics or malefics. The interpretation can be different depending on who is and what is brought into play. Then, complex networks of relations, which can be like chess play, are developed. I will present one example (it is made as simple as possible) in order to encourage students to do research further on. Libra is on the ascendant. The ruler of the ascendant (Venus) was in the 11th field of the sign of Leo. Venus is in conjunction with Mercury (the ruler of the 12th field) of orb 5. Meanwhile, Mercury is retrograde. Mars is in Leo in the exact conjunction with the Moon, only 3 degrees from the conjunction of Venus and Mercury. Mars rules the 7th field (marriage) and the 2nd field (money). The Moon rules the 10th field – career, business...

It is the horoscope of a friend of mine, and I will not offer his natal chart in order to protect his privacy. On this occasion, I will help you understand this stellium and how it is reflected on everyday life.

Firstly, we will study Venus, which rules the ascendant – it is in Leo in the 11th field. The Natus is extrovert, full of energy (fire sign), sociable and optimistic (11th field). He is focused on money, status, the fruits of career, reputation (11th field, Leo). Thus, since Leo is accentuated and 11th field, as well, we conclude that the natus is not a retiring person. On the contrary, he is brimming with energy. He meets people gladly, he is friendly...

Venus is in conjunction with Mercury in Leo – it additionally supports what we have just mentioned – the natus has a young spirit, his face seems as if he was a few years younger, he is interested in books, information, and he is curious, prone to research...

However, Mercury is retrograde and comes from the 12th house. It is, however, a negative side of Mercury because it comes from the house, which signifies illness, anxiety, problems, prisons, spiritual suffering, isolation... The natus (Venus) grew up at his grandparents' because his parents left him when he was a little boy (12th field). So, he did not have a normal upbringing, his Grandma and Grandpa took care of him. Obviously, he was not much interesting to his parents. As Venus rules the ascendant (head), and Mercury rules the 12th field of the horoscope, the natus occasionally suffers from severe headache and has problems with sinuses. Venus also builds a conjunction with Mars (which rules the 7th field). The natus can be proud of strong love relationships that lasted long (Leo-the fixed sign). As Mars presses with its conjunction the ruler of the ascendant (Venus), here we see the sports nature, and that he is active in various sports. However, although everything is so, love life is imbued with a lot of anxieties because Venus signifies partnership and love, and Mars is not a friend with Venus – conjunction of Venus and Mars postpones the marriage and contributes to love suffering. Furthermore, Mars is in conjunction with the Moon, and we have already said that the Moon rules the 10th house – the natus occasionally suffers from the disease of joints and knees which is presented by the 10th house. As the Moon signifies house and mother, it describes frequent moving and a very crude mother (Mars-Moon conjunction). This conjunction also gives the chance that mother lives longer than father, because in this example the Sun is somewhat weaker.

On the other side, we have the combination – Venus (the ruler of the ascendant) in conjunction with Mercury (the ruler of the 12th field), Mars (the ruler of the 7th field) and the Moon (the ruler of the 10th field) in the 11th field of the horoscope. This indicates that the natus works in public (the 1st house, 7th house + 10th house of the horoscope) and that he has made a lot of money (11th field in the sign of Leo). Conjunction of Venus and Mercury contributed to the fact that the natus is engaged in writing a little – he has published two poetry books for children (Mercury conjunction Venus) and one drama (Mercury in Leo). As Mercury (children, books, school...) is in conjunction with Venus, Mars and the Moon, we doubt that the natus has more children, which is true. All these planets from the 11th field "look at" the 5th field (children). Mercury (the ruler of the 12th field) is in conjunction with Mars – the natus thinks quickly and often interrupts other while speaking (rash, slightly nervous) and often comes into conflicts with younger people (Mercury). As Mercury is retrograde, it comes from the 12th field and builds a conjunction with malefic Mars (which comes from the 7th field – partner) – we find out that the natus's partner adopted one child from Africa before their marriage (retro Mercury from the 12th field) and brought him into marriage. If we continued researching, we would come to unbelievable revelations and discoveries. However, I have already mentioned that a stellium creates a very rich network of relationships, which can be more complex than a chess board. The aim is that the astrology practitioner understands how some planetary relations can simultaneously bring bad and good results and to live in the natus mixed in such a way. So, nothing is absolutely white and clean, nor is everything black, bad and morbid. Planetary relations are intertwined, bringing certain quality and challenges, as well as hardships, which the natus has to overcome (nobody will do that instead of him). There are a lot of factors in the horoscope of my friend, which additionally support certain facts, but we have tried to deal with the stellium of planets. Sometimes it can happen that all planets in the stellium act simultaneously, sometimes one is more dominant and stronger, and sometimes a planetary influence is not felt at all. All these should be studied carefully. The more you work and research, the better you will be.

*Which is the strongest planet in the stellium?*

It is often the planet, which has the strongest dignity. For example, Venus, Moon, Mars and Uranus are in conjunction in the sign of Libra. Venus has the strongest influence, when it is in its own sign – it is the ruler, but unfortunately, it endures ill-fated influence of two malefics.

I also recommend that you should transfer the horoscope, which you are researching, into the equal system of houses (no matter whether you use Koch's system, the Placidus system or some other system in practice). The planet which is closest to the top of the house, in which the stellium is, has the strongest influence, but it does not have to be positive. For example:

Ascendant is on the 14th degree of Scorpio (use the system of equal houses!). In the fifth field there is Mercury (16th degree of Pisces) in conjunction with Venus (19th degree of Cancer), the Sun (21st degree of Pisces) and Mars (23rd degree of Pisces). In this case, Mercury has the strongest influence because it is closest to the top of the 5th house, which begins on the 14th degree of Pisces. Thus, Mercury has the strongest influence, but all other planets also strongly influence the same house (Do not forget that we have used the equal system of houses).

Some astrologers use this order when they determine the strength of Stellium:

The planet, which rules the stellium, is the strongest planet (for example Mars in Scorpio, the Sun in Leo, etc.).

The planet, which is exalted in stellium, is the second according to its strength (Mars in Leo, the Sun in the sign of Sagittarius...).

If personal planets, chronocrators (Saturn and Jupiter) and transcendental planets are found, then personal planets are always stronger and they color the stellium (for example, the Moon is in conjunction with Saturn, Uranus and Pluto...).

If planets are weakened in its basic dignity, then they cannot rule the stellium in any case (for example: the Moon in Capricorn, Mars in Libra, Mercury in Pisces...).

## Mutual reception

Two planets are in mutual reception, when both are in the changed domicile – for example: Mercury is in Libra, and Venus is in the sign of Gemini. In that way, they are connected with its dispositor in a special way. In other words, although it may seem that planets are weak or modestly placed, they still have the power, which will, quite certainly, be expressed. Mutual receptions can be very strong, such as Mars in Leo and the Sun in Aries, and they can also be formed by weak planets, for example, Mars in Cancer and the Moon in Scorpio or Venus in Scorpio, Mars in Taurus etc. Medieval astrologers wrote books about mutual reception (Guido Bonatti and others), and also a lot of information can be found in the "Christian Astrology" by William Lilly.

Mutual reception is especially important in horary astrology. A practitioner will understand this topic better when he/she starts studying horary astrology.

This is the horoscope of the best tennis player of all times, Roger Federer. Virgo is on the ascendant, which is often focused on diligent and devoted work, modesty, self-denial, smart decisions, caution... Federer is very reserved, cultured, balanced, and tactical; it is hard to read on his face what he thinks or feels... The ruler of the ascendant is Mercury in Leo in conjunction with the Sun in the 12th field – Leo strives for success, recognition, and Mercury with the Sun supports this affirmation. A strong twelfth house speaks about the fact that although he is a well-known star, Federer lives in a quiet and reserved way with his family. Also, the 12ᵗʰ house influences the humanitarian work and compassion – Federer is known as a man, who donated great money to hungry children in Africa. Such a horoscope contains favorable and unfavorable components. One should immediately notice that even three planets are in their fall – Venus, Mars and the Moon. They are responsible for the emotional side of life, showing of emotions, family life, mother, marriage and many other things. This is an excellent example, where planets in fall brought great business and financial success. In the background there is hard work, and self-denial, as well as great devotion to what he does. We notice that the Sun is extremely strong (in the sign of its domicile) and that Saturn is very strong in its sign (exaltation). However, we will not deal with the horoscope in detail, but with the mutual reception.

Example number 1.

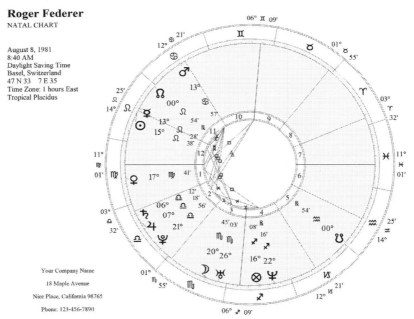

**Roger Federer**
NATAL CHART

August 8, 1981
8:40 AM
Daylight Saving Time
Basel, Switzerland
47 N 33   7 E 35
Time Zone: 1 hours East
Tropical Placidus

Mars is very weak in the sign of Cancer in the 11th field and it builds a square towards Saturn, Jupiter and Pluto. Such a weak Mars can influence financial affairs and health in a bad way, as well as the life of parents, sexual energy etc. However, the Moon is in the sign of Scorpio next to the fixed star Kiffa Borealis, which often speaks of successful and famous people (that does not have to be the rule), and it is in mutual reception and in trine with the above mentioned, very weak Mars. Such a mutual reception makes Mars strengthened together with the Moon and thus, they protect the houses, which they rule and inhabit – Mars protects family and father, and Mars protects mother and his wife. In this case, parents stayed together, and Federer is well-known as the family man, who nurtures family values – they all travel together to tennis tournaments, family is numerous and happy... Certainly, planets in fall will inflict some kind of damage, but mutual reception helps this damage to be less, and positive effects to be seen in all these.

Example number 2.

**Alain Delon**
NATAL CHART

November 8, 1935
3:25:08 AM
Standard time
Sceaux, France
48 N 47   2 E 17
Time Zone: 0 hours West
Tropical Placidus

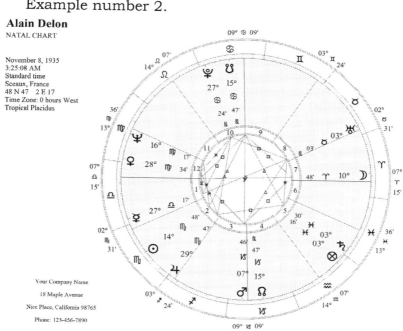

Alain Delon was born with the ascendant in the sign of Libra. Libra is primarily focused on art, relations with people, emotional relationships, love affairs, film, music etc. In any case, a person with the ascendant in Libra can never live alone – they always need others in order to feel well. In the field of partnership, the Moon is in Aries, and the ruler of the house of marriage is the strong Mars in the square with the same Moon – many partners were emotionally hurt, there were scandals, stress...

Alain Delon is presented by a very weak Venus – it is in the 12$^{th}$ field close to the very degree of its fall. Therefore, the ruler of the ascendant is extremely weak – Delon had a beautiful perception of himself all his life, and also he talked about himself using superlatives, how he was the most attractive, the most handsome man and similar... The position in the 12$^{th}$ field influences the character weakly – he made friends with petty thieves, and later in life with criminals; he was at the center of scandal when his bodyguard from Belgrade was killed and alike. Weak Venus speaks of emotional relations, marriage and alike – Delon had numerous relationships which ended ingloriously. The well-known actress, Romy Schneider, supposedly, tried to take her own life because of Delon. In brief, although he was an attractive and handsome man, he did not have a way with women. What was his growing up like?

Mars in exaltation in square with the Moon, which is the natural signifier of family, is on the top of the 4$^{th}$ field (family). Parents abandoned Delon when he was four, in order to come back to him when he became famous. Delon used to mention that the lack of family in his childhood colored his character and behavior towards women pretty much.

When we return to the ruler of the ascendant, we think that this man does not have chance, taking into consideration the fact that Venus rules the ascendant (health, duration of life, character, strength...). The position of Venus in the 12$^{th}$ field close to the degree of its fall additionally supports these doubts. However, Venus is in mutual reception with Mercury (which is its dispositor), and therefore, Venus after extreme weakness in time becomes strong (its dispositor is in the sign where Venus is in the domicile) – from a problematic boy Delon became a super-star and probably one of the most famous people in the world. His popularity was so great that a man needs one voluminous book in order to conjure that up for a reader. He acted in numerous films; he lived an incredible life and earned millions of dollars only on the basis of his name and physical appearance. Of course, his character never changed much, so we do not know him as a wise man, spiritual teacher or motivational speaker – he is still full of self-confidence and in love with himself or the memory on what he used to be. Thus, here we have seen again how mutual reception brings great results. In order to make it clear, not everyone will become famous actors and tennis players, but in the horoscopes of other people, mutual reception will also mean great help and support.

## Final dispositor of the horoscope

Final dispositor of the horoscope is the planet which disposits all other planets and is in its domicile. If there are two or more planets in one horoscope, which are in the sign of their domicile, then you are well on the way to conclude how that horoscope does not have a final dispositor. The same goes for the horoscope, which does not have a planet in its domicile. Final dispositor can give great results in the field, which it rules or make other planets be corrected and "cured" through it, if they are weak or attacked. I have worked with a man, in whose horoscope the Sun was the final dispositor. He grew up without parents on the street, he did not have any formal education, nor was he loved, he lived in poverty... However, over time he developed into a fantastic person, who has a lovely family, earns a lot of money, travels... Also, he instigated a few spiritual schools around Europe, whose idea is to spread consciousness and any type of spiritual progress. In his middle age he expunged meat from his nutrition and got interest in ayurveda. It is a man, who had a horrible childhood, hard life... Thus, final dispositor can bring relief and relaxation if life conditions were not wonderful. Final dispositor takes all the worries on itself and it is capable of compensating for what the person did not get naturally on his birth. For the example of visualization of final dispositor, take a strong, branchy tree, which is young and healthy. Also, imagine that on the ground, where that tree grows, terrible winds whip and there are monsoon rains – in spite of that terrible weather and harsh climate, the tree is strong and healthy, and it can resist all gusts of wind and rain. This is precisely what the final dispositor in somebody's horoscope is. This is one example of the horoscope with final dispositor.

Example:

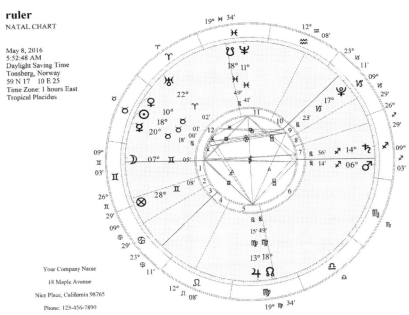

**ruler**
NATAL CHART

May 8, 2016
5:52:48 AM
Daylight Saving Time
Tonsberg, Norway
59 N 17   10 E 25
Time Zone: 1 hours East
Tropical Placidus

How can one come to Venus as a final dispositor of the horoscope?

Let's start from the Moon. It is in the sign of Gemini; its dispositor is Mercury in Taurus, and Mercury's dispositor is Venus. Thus, here one of the circles ends. The Sun is also in the sign of Taurus, and dispositor is again Venus. Jupiter is in the sign of Virgo, its dispositor is Mercury, and Mercury's dispositor is Venus, as we have just mentioned. Mars and Saturn are in Sagittarius, their dispositor is Jupiter and its dispositor is Mercury. Mercury's dispositor is Venus. From this we see that all planets are going to flow into one planet, which is particularly strong – and that is Venus. Let's take a look at this Venus. It is in the sign of its domicile (Taurus), exceptionally fruitful and well-aspected – it builds a strong sextile with Neptune, conjunction with Mercury (one of the codes for art) and conjunction with the Sun (the other code for art). All this is in the 12th field, which also speaks about art and talents (especially because they are benefics). Venus also builds a strong trine with Jupiter and Pluto. Considering the fact that Venus is the final dispositor in the sign of Taurus, it is probably a future artist because the Moon (popularity, crowds, public life...) is on the ascendant, and the ruler of the 10th field (occupation, career, what we will become...) is in the 7th field (public). The father of the child is also an artist (the Sun in conjunction with Venus and Mercury in the 12th field and all this in trine towards Pluto and Jupiter). Mother (the Moon) is a doctor (the Moon in opposition to Mars and Saturn, and in square with Neptune and Jupiter). In order to be more confident about this, I have to write that this child adores music, dances and sings a little bit, although it has only 20 months. Of course, in the domain of what children of that age can do. Thus, whatever the natus decides to do in life, Venus will pull it up and determine its final destiny. It does not have always to be good, but sometimes it turns out to be better than parents had expected.

36862774R00115

Made in the USA
San Bernardino, CA
24 May 2019